T0113551

BEFORE THEIR TIME

BEFORE THEIR TIME
WOMEN
WHO DARED

SHIRLEY H. WELLS

Copyright © 2023 Shirley H. Wells.

All rights reserved. No part of this book may be used or reproduced by any means, graphic, electronic, or mechanical, including photocopying, recording, taping or by any information storage retrieval system without the written permission of the author except in the case of brief quotations embodied in critical articles and reviews.

This book is a work of non-fiction. Unless otherwise noted, the author and the publisher make no explicit guarantees as to the accuracy of the information contained in this book and in some cases, names of people and places have been altered to protect their privacy.

Archway Publishing books may be ordered through booksellers or by contacting:

Archway Publishing
1663 Liberty Drive
Bloomington, IN 47403
www.archwaypublishing.com
844-669-3957

Because of the dynamic nature of the Internet, any web addresses or links contained in this book may have changed since publication and may no longer be valid. The views expressed in this work are solely those of the author and do not necessarily reflect the views of the publisher, and the publisher hereby disclaims any responsibility for them.

Any people depicted in stock imagery provided by Getty Images are models, and such images are being used for illustrative purposes only.
Certain stock imagery © Getty Images.

Interior Graphics/Art Credit: Tracy Ruge-Folks

ISBN: 978-1-6657-4847-6 (sc)
ISBN: 978-1-6657-4848-3 (e)

Library of Congress Control Number: 2023915201

Print information available on the last page.

Archway Publishing rev. date: 09/18/2023

CONTENTS

INTRODUCTION

Nothing in life is to be feared, it is only to be understood. Now is the time to understand more, so that we may fear less."
—*Marie Curie*

Books are written about famous or infamous people – royalty, presidents, prime ministers, dictators, leaders, successful artists, writers, poets, actors and singers. Biographies are also written about generals, war heroes, the wealthy, nobility and even murderers. Out of the hundreds of thousands of words written about widely known people, a few, very few, were written in the past about women. Women were not ordinarily recognized for great acts of leadership, heroics, artistic or scientific achievement, wealth or great evil.

The history of men is fairly well documented. The famous ones led fascinating, dynamic lives, riddled with tales both heroic and destructive. Biographers have researched and written widely about those who led or shaped history. Art, literature and film have preserved the lives and stories of the men who defied the odds and defined their times.

Women were seldom worthy of that kind of study; they were not movers and shakers. Other than a few royal women such as Cleopatra of Egypt, Elizabeth I of England, Catherine the Great of Russia, Queen Isabella of Spain or Joan of Arc, females seldom ruled or influenced their historical time. These indomitable women were anomalies in their time, but they blazed a trail for others to later emulate. However, most women of those times in history never even hoped to attain any power or equality.

Throughout history, women have been repressed, subjugated and relegated to secondary roles. To my great shock, Neanderthals may have lived in a true era of equal rights for women. Both male and female were ever on the quest for survival, and anthropologists have discovered that these cave dwellers shared the many responsibilities necessary for their survival. These early beings had to work as a team, had to form a partnership to live and protect their young. Both men and women hunted, made their weapons, gathered edible plants, made the body coverings which served as clothing and shared numerous tasks. Neanderthals lived primarily in small family groups. As they moved from cave to cave, it was necessary for both sexes to protect the young and the old. It was the earliest period of seeming male/female equality. Why did this partnership evolve into a male dominated society which has lasted for thousands of years?

Neanderthals, because of small numbers, had to interbreed; they were also found to universally have been wounded and killed by the wild animals they hunted and lived among. Their young seldom survived childhood in harsh living conditions; plus, there were many diseases which were deadly to this species. It is generally agreed that their early ancestors had migrated from the south to the north as they followed the animal herds. By the end of the ice age, many Neanderthals lived in northern colder climates. When the Homo Sapiens started migrating from Africa into the northern territories, there was interbreeding with the Neanderthals who completely disappeared 40,000 years ago after surviving their dangerous lives for at least 430,000 years.

It was the Homo Sapiens who first stopped their wanderings to settle down and start planting and growing their food. This fostered a new competition as they felt the need to guard and "own" their crops, animals and land. It appears that this was the beginning of the loss of women's equality. Somehow, new roles were defined and demanded of females. This has been the legacy of millions of women for thousands of years.

One would have hoped that those humans following primitive cavemen were more enlightened and treated women as intelligent, capable and valued human beings, but alas. History reveals that women were ever the helpmates not the dominant adults in all societies. Why did the world societies become patriarchal, with men dominating countries, communities, homes and the women who lived in them?

Women, for the most part, have lived and died in obscurity, linked only to their subservient roles in men's lives. The one major goal established for all females was marriage. Jane Austin and other authors echoed this theme repeatedly. Girls had few choices and were forced by laws to be reliant on men. Their lives were constrained by the demands of the time: maintain the homes, bear and raise children and care for their husbands and parents. Little else was recognized or tolerated, even in recent history. As for the men, other than sex, what was their great attraction to marriage. At least, for those more affluent families, they offered a dowry to the man who would marry their daughter. At times, this was a considerable fortune. Looks, mutual interests, attraction be damned -- dowries, money was what was important – men proposed, married and prospered with their newfound fortune.

Once married, men were supposed to be strong and protective of the females in their homes, but many men did not follow this stricture. Women have always "belonged" to the men in the homes – their fathers, their husbands, their male guardians. How women and children were treated within the home was always a secret. Abuse was widespread but only whispered about and always tolerated. The victims tended to die early.

Women's roles were quite clearly defined: daughter, wife, mother, housekeeper, caretaker, nurse, role model for the girls. Women who dared to defy their roles were vilified, ridiculed and ostracized. Their talents, creativity and abilities were ignored on the world stage. A few, very few, resisted those highly limiting expectations.

It is fascinating to learn about women's lives and roles throughout history. In early Greco-Roman times, at least there were goddesses for women to worship and emulate. Men of that time learned that you don't want to mess with an angry goddess, because stories of male gods attempting to do so were not promising. I like to think that women of that era would remind repressive males that they were praying to a goddess for protection. Hopefully, that would have given pause to any abuse contemplated. In those times, cultures were rather uninhibited and hedonistic, but once again, men ruled, women followed.

Biblical times seemed even less promising for women. Society was ruled by the Church of the country. In Europe, that was the Roman Catholic Church which taught fear of God and his retribution if one strayed from a pious path. Most religions acknowledged one God. That God did not seem to be interested in women as individuals or as a group. According to the texts of those times, all the world's religions fairly ignored women's contributions in their writings, their liturgy and their holy books. Below is one personal example of the bewilderment this lack of recognition incurred in my young self.

I was a young church-going attendee of our near-by protestant church. I was treated kindly there and enjoyed the many activities provided. I learned that the Bible was "Holy" and contained the word of God. When I was 11 years old, I was a prolific but indiscriminate reader. Comic books, books written for boys, books written for girls, classics or adult books, they all held my interest. Sunday school lessons and church sermons convinced me that I was a lost soul if I did not study and believe the Holy Bible. I was somewhat disenchanted with the beginning of the Christian Bible which began with something akin to a family tree.

In the first book of the Bible, the book of Genesis, there was a litany of male names, starting with Enoch who "begat" his son, Erad. This was followed by an endless list of male names each introduced with a "begat". It appeared that these truly remarkable men "begat" all the males in this line. What a feat! Apparently, no women were involved.

Also remarkable is that those men never "begat" any daughters – no pesky wives or daughters, just men begetting sons. Very impressive – to bear children all by themselves. This first strange detail partly derailed my interest in reading this massive tome, but I continued to be taught other Bible stories.

According to these Biblical stories, it seems that women were either saints (very few of these), dutiful wives, slovens or prostitutes. Interesting categories; but I noted that the Bible, both the old and new Testaments, were written entirely by men. Since I could not recognize any saints, slovens or prostitutes in my small, midwestern world, I was confused by women's evolution into the housewives of my generation.

I later found that Biblical women not only had been erased as mothers, but were considered to be incapable of telling the truth (liars). In those times, if a woman was accused of adultery (by a man who, naturally, always told the truth), she would be stoned to death. What a convenient way to get rid of a no-longer sexy wife. Men of the day -- religious, yes; spiritual, not quite.

The fall of the Roman Empire started in the 4th Century. The Medieval Period lasted around 1,000 years, beginning around 500 A.D and lasting until close to 1500 A.D. The early Medieval period is viewed as chaotic and lawless, but it is also a time of religious crusades and the code of chivalry. The feudal system dominated this time with castles and manors providing protection to the dependent workers and their families in exchange for their working the fields and taking care of the nobility and the wealthy. As the Roman Empire crumbled, new nations were established, including England, France and Spain. Germany and Italy became city-states. In the latter years of Medieval times (1300 – 1500), the invention of gunpowder intensified the brutality of war. Yet literature often depicts a romantic view of brave and chivalric knights defending the righteous and the helpless women.

Women were still seen as property, but the kindlier men of the time enacted a progressive law to help save women from being beaten to death by the men in their lives, which had been a quite acceptable thing to do. This law was called the "Rule of Thumb" and stated that a man could only use a stick no larger than the width of his thumb to beat his women, hopefully keeping them bruised and broken, but alive. This was thought to be a revolutionary and compassionate step forward for the women of the time. Men were "wardens and protectors of women". I am uncertain as to how grateful the women might have been to have a "warden" and be protected in this brutal manner.

The printing press was invented during the late Medieval times, and by 1500 A.D., 40,000 books had been printed in fourteen European countries. Unfortunately, only boys of the nobility were taught to read, so obviously women of the time could not even enjoy this distraction. It was demanded of Medieval women that they be unerringly chaste, and if they were assaulted, it was dangerous to reveal anything. Women never accused the rapist of this violence, although rape was rampant in those times. The reason for this bitter silence was that if a woman revealed her assailant, then her father, husband or other male relative had to duel the accused rapist. If her rapist lost the duel, he was deemed guilty and put to death. If the woman's male champion lost the duel, she was deemed guilty of lying and was then burned at the stake. A movie called "The Last Duel" was recently made about one such true historical case. Obviously, if the men in the victim's family were not well known for their dueling skills, she would be reluctant to make an accusation. By now, one does yearn for the laws of Karma to go to work. May all the men of those times reincarnate as women.

The 14th to the 17th centuries ushered in the Renaissance – the Age of Enlightenment". The Age of Enlightenment involved great strides forward in the arts, science, engineering and mass- produced goods. The central doctrine emphasized individual liberty and religious tolerance. A primary belief was that human history is a record of progress. Life, liberty and property rights were a critical part of this emerging philosophy. The American Revolution was greatly influenced by this approach.

Amazingly, one of the tenets of the Renaissance was that women were to have equality. However, the brilliant light in "Enlightenment" was pretty dim when it shone on women's equality. Beliefs by most men about women's intelligence, abilities and capabilities remained low. Women were still unable to hold public office or make decisions regarding public policy, law or property.

This enlightened time also did not include the abolishment of the mistreatment of women. In the Renaissance, men became enlightened, women's light continued to be extinguished.

From the Renaissance to the late Victorian age, women could not inherit property if there was any male relative claimant. If a woman's husband died and there was an estate, the wife and her daughters would need to move from their home and be under the control of other relatives or the male who inherited their former home. Since this was also called the age of courtliness and the Age of Reason, hopefully the males in the family would take pity on their homeless female victims of this repressive law. Fortunately, for women, life spans were short in those times. Malnutrition shortened life expectancy to 35 years in France, 40 years in Great Britain, a bit longer in the U.S. At least women didn't have to suffer a long life of neglect and humiliation; they died early.

The Industrial Revolution (1760 to 1840) began in Great Britain and spread to America and throughout the world. The textile industry was the first to be mechanized. This revolution took production from hand-made to machinery-made. It soon mechanized factory production. As factories started manufacturing more types of goods, employers were looking for cheap labor.

Men, women and children worked for starvation wages in unsafe conditions and had no labor rights. They were forced to work six days a week for 10 to 12 hour a day. For women, between taking care of their homes, children and husband and working long days, they had no life. If one was injured by the unsafe practices and conditions, there was no compensation, no health care, no assistance in any way. Because jobs were easy to find for the uneducated, the standard of living did increase for the general population. This did not mean that women's lives were improving; it meant that many now had two jobs instead of one. So much for progress.

Early in the 20th century, many women in England and America started seriously rebelling. They demanded equal pay, equal rights. They demanded the right to vote. Most men of the time, and their elected, all-male leaders, were horrified and angry at the audacity of these women. The men wanted the status quo to remain firmly in place. Women were arrested and jailed for protesting. Lawmakers refused to acknowledge their rights. It took years of punishment, vilification and humiliation before these brave women finally won PART of their agenda. On August 18, 1920, they were allowed to vote. An about face by society in their treatment of women? Not quite.

Today, in the U.S.A. women who often do the exact same job as men make less money. Lawmakers in some states still refuse to ratify the Equal Rights Amendment. Even more horrifying to women throughout the country, the Supreme Court, as of 2022, reversed a 50-year ruling protecting a woman's right to choose. Legislators in the states (primarily male) get to decide what girls and women are allowed to do and to be. Men, of course, are still free in many places to impregnate a female and then walk away from all responsibility. Chivalry is not dead, but it is rather badly wounded.

Another alarming trend is that the U.S. federal courts are attempting to restrict women's rights, and many states are passing laws to further negate any progress already gained by women. Most of the women of today are horrified at the erosion of their hard-fought demands for recognition as equal human beings. Like the women of the early 20th century, they march, they demand, and they vote. These women will not tolerate the old patriarchal power plays and will continue to insist on a life for themselves outside of the stereotypical role many women have been forced to live.

> *"I don't want my pain and struggle to make me a victim. I want my battle to make me someone else's hero."*
> —*Anonymous*

Yes, progress has been made. Women now hold positions of leadership and power in the workplace and in the government. Women with power are still a minority, but the numbers are growing. Hopefully, these female leaders can prevent the complete erosion of women's rights that some males are trying to impose on all females.

The women I have highlighted in this book have been largely overlooked in the history books, but they should not be forgotten because each has helped forge a step toward future improvements in women's lives. There is hope in the stories of the women I have chosen to return to our consciousness. They existed, they lived, they prevailed. These women moved beyond doubt, beyond fear in a time when the restrictions to their freedom were even more difficult to attain than now.

Yet, they survived, they strengthened. They lived their lives on their own terms and refused to be categorized in a role that did not fit their bold personalities. None allowed themselves to be cast aside by society's norms and expectations.

Each of them shined a light for others in their own generation and for those of us who followed. They created possibilities for others with courage and determination to overcome personal barriers and personal circumstances to achieve, to succeed and to triumph over expectation, judgement and obstacles. These women inspire us to dream and to visualize our own possibilities and talents. They are role models, icons, examples. We must never forget their impact on the past, the present and the future. Once overlooked and forgotten, they are the models for every individual's determination to shape their own future.

Yes, the women I write about are heroines; they remind us of our innate search for our own unique path. Ultimately, they are us – women seeking insights, women seeking to free themselves from other's expectations and criticism. As you search for new insights into your own truths – allow your light to be shone forward for future females.

NEFERTITI

═══════

*"The point of power is always in the present moment.
This is where we begin to make changes."*

—*Louise Hay*

═══════

For this small volume, I have attempted to select women who were ahead of their time, and Nefertiti was one of the very first that history has acknowledged as unusual, unique and daring.

This book has been designed in an historical context. Nefertiti who was born in 1370 B.C. and died in 1330 B.C. in Thebes, Egypt is my most ancient subject. She lived 3700 years ago, and her life demonstrates that even that far back certain women could rise above the normal lives of their contemporaries to heights that were unheard of both then and now. Nefertiti was the royal wife of Akhenaten, the Pharoah. For unknown reasons, he relied on her so heavily, he had her elevated to co-ruler of Egypt. After her husband's death, she ruled exclusively until her son (or possible grandson), Tutankhamun came of age and ascended the throne. During her tenure as sovereign, she made decisions which changed the history of Egypt. Why does Nefertiti hold first place in the history of women? First, a review of the Egypt of 3700 years ago.

Ancient Egyptians worshipped a multitude of gods and goddesses. The relationship of these gods and goddesses was complex and confusing. The Egyptians of the time lived much shorter lives than modern man, and their worship of the deities reflected the hazardous and unpredictable lives they lived. These deities helped them maintain a sense of order and

1

well-being in their lives. Because they believed that death was a new beginning to the next life which was similar to the life they were living, they needed these gods and goddesses to guide them into the next life which, hopefully, would be a better one. These beings were a way of explaining the unknown. Many offerings were made to the deities in order to appease and please them so that they would continue to protect and guide their followers.

The ancient Egyptians also believed that the afterlife would be much like life on earth. Their tombs had painted scenes on the walls recreating the life they had lived. This has provided future generations with much knowledge of the everyday life in ancient Egypt. Most Egyptians believed that their king (Pharoah) was a god. Others seemed to believe that the king could relate to the gods in a very special way. This belief demanded that the Pharaoh be treated with respect and absolutely obeyed because he was the bridge to the gods. Most Egyptians were in awe of their ruler.

The Nile River was the life blood of Egypt both before and after that time. The population lived along its shores as it provided transportation, food and the water which sustained life. The pharaohs had absolute power over everyone, including their royal and noble families. Each pharaoh had his own stable of wives. Only one of these women would be designated as Royal Wife, and she was the one who ruled the household. Nefertiti was selected early to be that Royal Wife and was probably a pre-teen when she was so chosen.

Life spans in those times were very short, for the ordinary men were put to work as boys building, maintaining and caring for the Pharoah's cities, fortifications and palaces. Few of these workers lived into their 20's. The Pharoah could live to the advanced age of 40+, but most died earlier. Females had much shorter lives because so many of these young girls and women died in childbirth. The death rate was very high among the females of Egypt.

The greatest power was in the hands of the pharaoh and his royal male relatives. Also wielding enormous power was the priest class which dominated the temples and the minds of their followers. There were a few women, very few, working in the temples. They were called priestess which meant "wife of the god". These women were usually married to the priests and were of high status. They frequently used music and dance to honor their gods. It was believed that Nefertiti had her education as a priestess. As for the other women of the time, their roles were pre-ordained by the men of all classes who ruled their country, their communities, their households and the women who lived in their homes.

Prior to Nefertiti, there had been two other female rulers of Egypt. Hatshepsut ruled after the death of her husband until her son attained manhood. She believed that the god Amun impregnated her human mother, thus she was divine. She ruled alone for seven years and then ruled jointly with her stepson, the Pharaoh. It was a successful and prosperous joint reign. However, unlike Nefertiti she never used the enormous power of her position to force change on her country.

Another female ruler was Neferusobek who was the last of her dynasty. Both of these women ruled temporarily. For Nefertiti, her ascension was entirely different. She was anointed as younger co-regent by her living husband and reigned with him while acting as chief administrator of Egypt. The other two women served as heads of state because of a too-young king. Nefertiti had her place as next female Pharoah secured by her experience and power as chief administrator of Egypt.

There is much mystery surrounding Nefertiti's birth, her life and her impact on history. Many well-known historians have written of her, and there is much controversy and debate among these professional historians about the details of her life. Little wonder that there are differing reports of what she accomplished 3,700 years ago when males dominated the landscape and females were not only powerless but totally expendable. Unlike other royal women of her time Nefertiti was so powerful and historically significant that much has survived to reveal the true nature and story of this remarkable woman.

I am not an historian nor an expert on ancient Egypt, and those that are cannot agree on her role in history. Because much has been lost in time, there is much disagreement about Nefertiti's life, her significant impact on history and her unbelievable power. Still, there was much to be learned from the many depictions of her in Egyptian art and in surviving papyrus accounts. I researched her and write of her because she intrigued me as a powerful woman in times when women typically did not wield power. Then and for centuries after, women were possessions, not intelligent, capable, creative beings. Egyptian wives had much shorter lives because, as stated before, so many of these young girls and women died in childbirth.

When I began this endeavor, I had scarce knowledge of Nefertiti. Her name was familiar to me only because I had heard that she was the mother of King Tutankhamun (King Tut). My criteria for selecting women I deemed ahead of their time was that their lives were unique and their actions exceeded all expectations for the era in which they lived. I was looking for great courage in their thinking, their decisions and their actions. Nefertiti met and exceeded all of my criteria.

What follows may not be absolutely accurate. If the Egyptian experts, the historians who have studied every surviving scrap of papyrus and every artistic representation, are still unsure, can the literal, the absolute true story be told in these pages? Perhaps not.

I will, though, relate those aspects of her life that most researchers seem to agree are accurate. The remaining text will, like the historians, reflect my best understanding of what transpired 3,700 years ago. I know that this rendering of Nefertiti's life is one that reflects my growing admiration and awe for this incredible woman who became a legend because she dared to use her talents and intelligence to become a powerful ruler.

As stated earlier, there were two other female rulers prior to Nefertiti; yet Nefertiti is the most controversial because of her role in history, her influence over her husband and her power as co-ruler and even ruler of her country. Of course, this leads to ongoing debates as to how this happened; how she rose in power and was given the role of administrator of Egypt. Her husband, Akhenhaten, became much hated because of his new religion and his economic excesses. Because of this, his name and Nefertiti's were erased from temples, shrines, buildings, tombs and written texts. This is unfortunate because as one author/historian wrote:

"More than any other Egyptian queen, it is Nefertiti who represents the epitome of true, successful female power that tapped into the emotions of her people, that embraced multiple perspectives, that reached out in a spirit of reconciliation to those who had been expelled or cast out. Ironically, in so doing she had to simultaneously morph into a masculinized king who is all but impossible to identify with Nefertiti the queen."

Nefertiti was born in 1370 B.C. in Thebes and died in 1330 B.C. in Thebes. It was generally agreed that Ay was the real father to Nefertiti. Ay's wife, Tey (titled, "Nurse of the Great Royal Wife), is acknowledged as her mother. Ay had been an army commander and had risen to power as royal chancellor and held the title "Superintendent of the Royal Horses". He was a very high official at the court of Akhenaten. It is believed he may have been related to the royal family by marriage. Ay had also acted as "God's father" to Akhenaten. It was generally agreed that it was Ay who guided Nefertiti on her path from co-ruler to sole kingship. He seemed to have her complete trust as she gained increasing power.

In order to put into context, the astonishing role Nefertiti played in this ancient time of great wealth and power in Egypt, the following brief glimpse of the history of the country is necessary. Also necessary is an overview of the controversial rule of Pharaoh Akhenaten who married and supported Nefertiti's unheard-of rise to power.

Each pharaoh had his own stable of wives who were young girls given to the Pharoah as gifts to gain influence and approval of the ruler. Only one of these young women would be designated as Royal Wife. Akhenaten selected Nefertiti to be his Royal Wife, so she was the one who ruled the household. Nefertiti was considered to be very beautiful and no doubt was also very intelligent and astute at how to please the Pharoah.

Akhenaten, the tenth ruler of the Eighteenth Dynasty was born in Thebes in 1352 B.C. to 1336 B.C. At birth he was named Amenhotep IV after his father, Amenhotep III. The administrative capital at this time was Memphis, and the greatest of the religious centers was Thebes.

His place of birth, Thebes, contained the largest and wealthiest temple complexes and the most powerful priesthood. These priests worshipped Amun who was considered to be the most important of the gods. Many historians believe that when the Amenhotep IV ascended to the throne, he was concerned with the growing wealth and influence of the priests of the time. He felt that they were gathering too much power and were attempting to take over the rule of Egypt. Because of the enormous offerings to the gods by the people, the priests had become extremely wealthy and were increasingly dictating the behaviors and actions of the general populace. Akhenaten felt this was only the prerogative of himself as Pharaoh.

Because of this, Amenhotep IV changed his name to Akhenaten to emphasize to the people that he was the son of Aten, the sun god, thus making himself a god. He also chose to alter the state religion and mode of worship by becoming the first ruler in history to name a monotheistic god, Aten. This radically changed the religion of the time. Many deities were worshipped prior to his ascendency to the throne, but he demanded that Aten be worshipped as the sole God.

In order to erase the old traditions of worship, ritual and art, the newly named Akhenaten moved the entire capital of Egypt from Thebes to a remote and empty site, selected, no doubt, because there was no existing religion in that area with its own god. He had this new city raised from nothing. There had not even been a village in this new location. He demanded that a huge city be built rapidly, overworking and killing thousands of craftsmen and laborers. As workers died from heat and exhaustion from slaving all day and night on his enormous temples, shrines and palaces, he demanded that these men and boys maintain an ever-greater killer pace to rapidly build the large city he planned.

In addition to the palaces and temples being built, Akhenaten had the laborers build houses of all sizes, administrative buildings, bakeries and factories. There was a total lack of care or empathy for the humans carrying out his harsh and unrealistic demands. All this was supposedly in honor of the one God – Aten, symbol of the sun. As the city builders died of heat and exhaustion, Akhenaten simply ordered new men be brought in to continue with his overwhelming demands. He was also demanding that all people only worship the one God he had chosen. This distressed the people of Egypt. The people hated both him and the new religion, but he was all powerful, and they did his bidding. It is estimated that the population of this new city grew to about 30,000 residents.

Nefertiti had been married to Akhenaten in Thebes and was with him during all this turmoil and radical change. She, of course, would have had no say in his decisions to re-take power from the priests and establish a new religion.

It is impossible to know if she agreed or disagreed with him at the time. Apparently, as a young girl she studied to be a priestess. Her father, Ay, then managed a marriage for her to the future pharaoh. Once married, she became a favorite of the future Akhenaten and thus became "Royal Wife". This certainly elevated her status, but what was it that Akhenaten relied on or needed from his favorite wife that allowed her to rise to ever greater heights?

One can only speculate about Nefertiti's life, her role in history and her personal power. Nefertiti was labeled "the Beautiful One Has Come, and the famous bust of her still viewed in a Berlin's Neues Museum would reenforce this view. When Akhenaten was still known as Amenhotep IV and living in Thebes, he had a temple erected in Karnak called the Mansion of the Benben, and it was dedicated to Nefertiti. Obviously, he had fallen in love with this beautiful woman. That, however, would not explain her increasing power over her court and her country.

What attributes, what talents, what abilities led him to trust and rely on Nefertiti so completely? Nefertiti bore Akhenaten six daughters in her seven or eight years as chief queen or Great Royal Wife. Strangely, if she did bear him a son, it would not have been recorded. For some unknown reason, men of the time recorded their daughters but not their sons. Was it superstition or fear of assassination or forgotten ritual that explained this? It is a mystery.

Very unusual for the time, Akhenaten positioned Nefertiti next to him in artists' rendering of his reign. He also commissioned many depictions of himself and Nefertiti in intimate situations. No other pharaoh had ever done this, for it was only gods and goddesses who were shown being sexually active. This was a clear message to Egypt's people that he and his queen were sacred and divine.

When their oldest two daughters became young girls, Akhenaten elevated Nefertiti to equal status with him, and he elevated their two oldest daughters to the position of Great Royal Wives. He was often depicted as caressing his little girls. Indeed, both of these daughters bore Akhenaten children. The oldest daughter of Nefertiti and Akhenaten, Meritaten died in childbirth, bearing her father's baby. There is an artistic rendition showing Akhenaten, Nefertiti and their other daughters mourning Meritaten after her death.

These incestuous relationships with daughters I found personally horrifying and ugly. In our modern world, the artistic rendition of the mourning parents would be seen as a cruel act of hypocrisy; but in the ancient world, where only royals married one another, these incestuous acts were understood and accepted.

As stated before, during the time that her daughters were elevated to royal wives, Nefertiti was equal in power in Egypt. This was never before done with any other royal wife. Her name was changed to reflect her new status, as had her husband's when he declared himself follower of Aten. These constant name changes have confused historians and led to debate about who was who. It must have been even more difficult for the people of Egypt.

Akhenaten and Nefertiti reigned at what was considered the wealthiest period of ancient Egyptian history. In order to establish his goal of one God, Akhenaten had moved his kingdom from the ancient Thebes to the newly established city he called Amarna. This new city contained several large open-air temples dedicated to Aten. Nefertiti and the rest of the royal family would have resided in the Great Royal Palace in the center of the city.

Of the many abuses perpetrated by the Pharoah Akhenaten, one great reform has benefitted the study of ancient Egypt. Artists were encouraged to portray the pharaoh in routine situations – being affectionate with Nefertiti, playing with his children. The art of the time also depicted nature and the ordinary lives of farmers. Historically, It has been deemed the finest era of Egyptian art. Akhenaten also changed the style and content of temple architecture.

What is most fascinating, there is historical evidence that Nefertiti, in her new role as a second powerful ruler, was the one who, according to the art depictions and papyrus remains, saw to the administration of Egypt. As such, she traveled throughout Egypt. Nefertiti is shown in many archeological sites as equal in stature to a king. In these depictions, she is seen doing things that only male royals would have done, such as killing Egypt's enemies, riding a chariot and worshipping Aten in the manner of a pharaoh. Of these, Nefertiti's battling the enemy is the most dramatic. Captive enemies decorated her throne; and this was unique to her. Battle was the prerogative of pharaohs, not their queens. Artists were instructed to paint Akhenaten and Nefertiti in equal power positions.

Once again, no other queen had ever been so portrayed. She was obviously highly intelligent and incredibly capable of taking on male roles of decision making and leadership. Her husband, Akhenaten, remained at home, ever more fanatical in his religious practices. Although he had created the world's first monotheistic religion, he became ever more fanatic and brutal in his insistence on his absolute rule over this unwanted religion. His plan to steer Egypt away from its myriad gods was unsuccessful with his people. This proto-monotheism changed Egypt's religion from a polytheistic religion to a monolatry which implied that there was one God to be worshipped, but he was not the only god. This shattered centuries of tradition in a religious revolution. Later rulers, who had returned to the old religion, considered him heretical and attempted to erase all references to him. Akhenaten and his religion were never popular with the priests, the other royals or the people of Egypt. He brought the vast, powerful and enormously wealthy Egyptian empire to the brink of collapse.

Akhenaten ruled for only 17 years. He died at close to age 50, which was a very old age at that time. Nefertiti was probably in her mid-twenties to early thirties when her husband died. She was now supreme ruler and immediately moved to refute her dead husband's tyrannical demands. Tutankhamun was only five or six years old, so Nefertiti became supreme ruler until he was old enough to claim the throne. Although historical records show the next king following Akhenaten's death was called by a different name, the majority of historians now accept that this was yet another name change for Nefertiti. It was common for new kings to adopt a new name.

Nefertiti's first audacious move was to return Egypt to its former religious belief systems. Aten was no longer sole god, Amun was newly reinstated as king of the gods, ruling over the many other gods worshipped by the priests and the people.

Some historians have identified the young Tutankhamun as the ruler who abandoned the city of Amarna to return to its old capital, Thebes. This would not have been possible as Tutankhamun was still a very young boy and not able to make such radical decisions. It seems logical that since Nefertiti was already co-ruler and had been running the country administratively that she would continue the reign until Tutankhaten became of age. This newly named Nefertiti/Smenkhkare/Neferneferuaten returned the treasures to their old temples, rehired priests, reinstituted divine offerings and attempted to heal old wounds inflicted by her dead husband.

She was not to live long enough to complete this difficult task. Nefertiti died in her late thirties in 1330 B.C. Although the famous King Tutankhamun ascended to the throne after her death, there is still argument over Nefertiti's relationship with him. Some historians firmly believe that King Tut was Nefertiti's son. Although all the pharaohs excluded the names or images of any male offspring, those opposed to the view of Nefertiti and Tutankhamun as mother and son refer to the genetic analysis of King Tut's mummy which indicated that he had been the product of incest. Since he was clearly named as next in line as pharaoh, this means he must be the product of Akenhaten and another royal wife. Since Nefertiti's daughters gave birth to their father's children, some believe that Tutankhamun is the child of one of Nefertiti's daughters who were Royal Wives, thus making King Tut the grandson of Nefertiti. If this is accurate, she is the only woman who became ruler of Egypt to have prepared her own son or grandson for the throne.

Whatever is true of Nefertiti's relationship with Tutankhamun, this much is absolutely true. She was first Royal Wife, she was co-ruler of Egypt, she reigned supreme over Egypt. She abandoned her husband's new religion, moved the capital back to Thebes and brought healing to a nation which had been torn asunder by Akenhaten. She was the only woman EVER to be depicted in battle dress fighting the enemy. Captive enemies decorated her throne. No other woman ever had that male role decorating her throne. That alone would have brought her fame, for women never, ever fought in battle – only men played that role. Once again, she changed history with her exploits.

Although Nefertiti lived 3,700 years ago, her life demonstrates that even in ancient times, a very few women did rise above the pre-ordained lives of their contemporaries to heights that were unheard of both then and now. Akhenaten relied on Nefertiti to be ruler in his name and make the important decisions as chief administrator of Egypt. When he died, she ruled exclusively and made decisions that changed the course of the history of Egypt. She dared to take on all male roles and take actions to improve the lives of its citizens. She was bold, fearless and amazing

Sadly, after Tutankhamun's death at age 19, Ay (Nefertiti's father, King Tut's grandfather) seized the throne. Ay reigned for only four or five years before his death. Tragically, Nefertiti's daughter had to become her father, Akhenaten's, Royal Wife. When he died, she was then married to Tutankhamun, her brother or half-brother. Then when he died early, she was forced to marry her grandfather, Ay. This girl was unable to escape the demands made on noble women of the time. They were forced to marry and obey the husbands of the time. Nefertiti was the sole woman to escape the unfortunate role of wife to any noble or ruler who demanded an incestuous marriage. Nefertiti was too powerful and maintained that power until her death in her late 30's. No other woman ever maintained that much control over her life 3700 years ago and for many thousands of years after. She set the standard for independence and provided the goal of equality for countless women who followed after.

NEFERTITI

ELIZABETH ANN FULLER

'I'd rather regret the risk that didn't work out,
than the chances I didn't take at all."

—*Simone Biles*

Why have I selected Elizabeth Ann Fuller, a woman lost in obscurity, lost in time as one of the women who was before her time? Why, because this woman, like many silent and unknown others who lived their quiet, heroic lives in obscurity, was extraordinary in her courage and daring. Like the reader, Elizabeth Fuller had never been known or heard of by this author. She was found entirely by accident, while doing research on a family tree. Once found, Elizabeth refused to die again, to be a footnote in a personal family history. Her bold move from England to an unsettled and dangerous land haunted me, and my recurring amazement at what she accomplished impelled me to write this book. She has demanded that her life and her time be acknowledged, be brought to the light. She was the inspiration for this book. This is my gift for you, my 11th great grandmother. This is your story.

Elizabeth Ann Fuller was born March 2, 1579 in Ivinghoe, Buckinghamshire, England. Like all of us, her family and community shaped her values and her actions. Her grandfather, Sir Nicholas Fuller, born 1515 in London, was a life-long rebel. He graduated from Christ College, Cambridge and became a barrister. As an attorney, he was constantly in trouble with the Crown and with the legal hierarchy. He often defended the members of a group that was then called Pilgrim

Separatists who wanted to reform the Church of England. These "separatists" wanted to ignore the world's concerns and dedicated themselves to Christianity as defined by the Bible. Sir Nicholas seemed to stand up for all who demanded equal rights with the wealthy and influential. His passion seemed to be equal rights for the common man. He also showed great contempt for the Church of England which he felt was corrupt. Sir Nicholas lived under the reigns of King Henry VIII, Edward VI, Queen Mary and Queen Elizabeth I. All were outraged by his defense of those who criticized the crown and his own assertions that the Crown should also be subject to all of the laws of the land.

As a result of his refusal to change in any way, he was repeatedly imprisoned in Fleet Prison in London. He would then defend himself by writing legal briefs based on citizen's rights. He would be freed, only to continue his arguments against the elite of the legal establishment, the nobility and the crown. His courageous refusal to ever recant any of his court arguments or his beliefs made him a pariah to all but those who secretly shared his belief in equality.

Chamberhouse Castle was his country home, and he moved his wife and seven children back and forth between there and London. One of his sons was Sir Cuthbert Dubbers Fuller (1542-1633) who was Elizabeth's father. How Cuthbert was influenced by his father's repeated conflicts and imprisonments, we know little; but many records show that he, too, was sent to Fleet Prison, and he died there. One can only conjecture as to how his father's constant battles with the hierarchy of England affected him politically, psychologically and socially, but we do know that he named one of his sons after his father, Nicholas. We also know that, like his father, he was sent to Fleet Prison. It would seem that he admired his father's actions and may have emulated them. This, in turn, would have influenced Elizabeth in various ways. What we know is her actions in their own way were as unusual and courageous as her father's and grandfather's.

Elizabeth's parents were Sir Cuthbert Fuller (1542-1633) and Elizabeth Laughton (1542-1579). She had two brothers, Sir Nicholas Fuller (1577-1620) and Jeremiah Geoffrey; plus, she had two half siblings, Christopher and Sarah. We know little of the family dynamics or their

travails as they lived in homes where family members had such obvious
passion for unwinnable causes.

Our first official record of Lady Elizabeth Ann Fuller is when she
married Sir Geoffrey (also called Jeffrey), Lord Mayor of London, around
1600. One wonders if a titled person holding the important office of Lord
Mayor would have married into a family whose reputation was often
reviled. There is no way of knowing when, precisely, all of the clashes
with the courts and the crown started; but it remains an interesting
question. Would he have married Elizabeth if this conflict was going on
at the time of their marriage?

What is certain is that Sir Geoffrey and Lady Elizabeth Ann had
five sons and two daughters in the nine years they were married, with
the first three born to them dying as toddlers. It is unimaginable what
anguish and grief this caused the parents, but surviving childhood was
problematical in the 1600's; as childhood diseases were, for the most part,
untreatable. Fortunately, the next four children survived into adulthood.
Their father, Sir Geoffrey Clements died in 1612 during an epidemic,
which may have been the plague. This left Elizabeth with three toddler
sons and an infant daughter. Apparently, because of the laws of the time
regarding progeniture, Geoffrey's older brother would have inherited the
family property and fortune, leaving Elizabeth with nothing. I initially
wondered why she did not take her children and go home to her parent's
home, but life may have been uncertain because of the turmoil there.

Geoffrey was a stockholder in the Virginia Land Company who
funded the first voyage to America in order to establish a permanent
settlement in the new world. He gave his shares of this land grant to
Elizabeth before he died. Whatever her motivation, Elizabeth decided
to take her tiny children and sail for Jamestown, Virginia to claim her
bequest. Elizabeth's first trip was in 1611, nine years before the famous
Mayflower sailed from England to Plymouth, Massachusetts in 1620.
All these passages to the new world were fraught with danger on the
old wooden ships of the times, and the trips took months to complete.
Elizabeth braved this hazardous trip with small children to care for and
no male to protect all of them once they arrived.

Jamestown has a fascinating history. It was founded by the Virginia Company in 1607 as the first permanent English settlement in the New World. That company had heard rumors of the mineral wealth already found in South America and wanted a permanent settlement from which they could launch exploration, discover valuable resources and expand on the land developed by the settlers. The Virginia Company recruited 104 men and boys to board the three ships chartered to sail the long four-month trip to the shores of the New World.

These adventurers left England in December, 1605 and landed on Jamestown Island on May 14, 1607. At the time, James I was King of England; and the settlers named the river on which they sailed inland after him. (James I became King following the long reign of Elizabeth I, his cousin) These new arrivals were looking for a permanent settlement location which would provide ultimate safety from the Spanish, who were at war with them. They found an island which had no Indians living on it; plus, it had the advantage of being surrounded on three sides with water, which made it defensible from Spanish attacks. They decided to name their settlement Jamestown after their king.

Many of the first settlers in 1607 were upper-class gentlemen unaccustomed to manual labor but hoping to make their fortune in this unexplored new world. There were few farmers or skilled laborers. There were few laborers who knew how to repair, how to build. The leader wrote to the Virginia Company begging that they send more craftsmen – not fortune seekers. However, within four to six weeks, by June, all working together managed to build a fort with cannons on all four sides. Some of the newcomers, disenchanted with the work involved, left to return to England on the ships which had brought new supplies and more men.

Initially, the Powhatan Indians living nearby were friendly and sent the new arrivals food because they had arrived with few supplies. Many Indians became unhappy because the area of Jamestown was also the hunting grounds for their tribe. In addition, the arrivals asked for more and more food and supplies. Finally, Powhatan had had enough and refused all requests. The three ships which had returned to England were supposed to return with supplies, but they were delayed more than a year. In addition to these threats to their survival, the new arrivals faced another danger. The waters newcomers were drinking was pulled from a brackish swamp, and it carried diseases of all sorts. Of even more danger were the plentiful mosquitoes in Jamestown; thus, malaria was prevalent. In 1608, the wife of one of the workers arrived; she was the first white woman to brave the dangers of the new land.

The years of 1609 and 1610 became known as the "starving time". Only sixty men of the 500 who had come to Jamestown survived those first two years. Eighty to ninety percent of the settlers died due to starvation and disease. Apparently, the one woman was not among the living. In May of 1610, supplies and new settlers arrived. Over 100 women trickled in after that, many were wives of the workers and craftsmen, or those willing to work for wages. As more and more settlers arrived and started spreading out over their lands, the Indian tribe became increasingly hostile to the intruders. This was their land and their hunting grounds.

The Virginia Company was growing impatient to see some profit from their investment. These pioneers had been introduced to the use of tobacco by the Indians, and one of the new settlers planted new strains of tobacco which became the cash crop for the settlement. When the first crop was sent back to England, the use of tobacco became wildly popular. It was being touted as a cure for coughs and a health benefit, so it started being widely used. The Virginia Company was finally getting a return on the money spent, and the Jamestown residents had a product which would make them solvent.

Elizabeth's husband, Geoffrey Clements, died in 1609, shortly after the birth of his daughter, Elizabeth. At that time, their son, Nicholas, would have been three years old and Jeremiah would have been two years old. Ezekial was only one year old at the time. The Compendium of American Genealogy, the Register of Maryland's Heraldic Families, and the Passenger and Immigration Lists Index all listed Elizabeth Clements, widow, as arriving in 1611 with her four children and one servant. She came to claim her land grant and returned to England. She sailed with her children and two servants again in 1617. This time she stayed to start a tobacco plantation on her land.

It seems certain from the records that Elizabeth's first trip to Jamestown with her three boys and infant daughter was 1611. Her initial motivation had to be the Virginia Land Grant that Geoffrey had left her. There was another interesting detail. One of Elizabeth's sisters was married to the captain of a ship which was commissioned to make return trips to America to bring settlers and supplies.

It was on that ship that Elizabeth sailed first to the new land which she hoped would provide security to her little family. I also believe that she found conditions unbearable in a settlement which was just recovering from disease and starvation.

The ship's manifest of 1617 stated that Elizabeth returned to Jamestown with her children in that year. They sailed on the ship named "George" which was captained by Elizabeth's brother-in-law and partly owned by her uncle. Her son, Nicholas would have been 11 years old, Jeremiah 10 years old, Elizabeth 8 years old and Ezekial 5 years old. She also brought two servants, a man, Jeffrie Hall, and a woman, Dorothy Greene. They arrived in Jamestown on June 10, 1617. She was known ever after for being the first "gentle woman" to arrive in America.

First woman or not, her daring to come to a wilderness with no male relative to protect her in this dangerous new land showed incredible courage. Unfortunately, it was the year of the great drought, coupled with a damaging hail storm which had wiped out the newly planted tobacco crops. Further, there were only five or six houses in Jamestown; the church had burned, and the bridge to the island was in dangerous disrepair. There were only about 350 people who had survived these disasters. Over 100 women had filtered in, primarily to join husbands or to be married; but none were considered "gentle women". Most of those early women had died during the "starvation time".

The 1617 move to America was permanent with only occasional visits to England. It is also unknown how she overcame all the hardships of these perilous times, but records show she survived and thrived. Two years after her arrival, in 1619, ninety women were recruited in

England to sail to Jamestown to become wives and start families. That same year, the first African slaves were brought to Virginia to work the tobacco fields. It was the beginning of the capture and enslavement of hundreds of thousands of Africans, and the great divide in America which eventually led to the Civil War and emancipation.

It is unknown, as yet, if Elizabeth was a part of this human tragedy, but it is known that she developed her land into a plantation starting in 1617. At that time, there were no slaves in America, so Elizabeth would have had to hire men to plant and harvest her tobacco crop. Hopefully, she remembered her family's history of defending the downtrodden and never used slaves.

Elizabeth did seem to be much admired. In 1620, John Clements Jr., who was a cousin by marriage, died and left Elizabeth his share of the ship "George". It was the ship she and her family had traveled on from England to Jamestown. This would have been a valuable asset for the young widow. In 1622, as more and more settlers encroached on Indian lands, the Powhatan Indians rebelled and attacked the outlying area where farmers were constantly expanding their territory. Approximately 1,200 people lived in these surrounding areas, and the Indians killed at least one third - 350 to 400 -of those living there. This began a long and bloody war with the Indians with troops sent from England to finally defeat the Indians with superior forces and weapons. Elizabeth and her children lived through all these fearful times.

Captain Ralph Hamor who had been educated at Oxford, was the captain of a group of English militiamen sent to protect the citizens of Jamestown. Elizabeth married him. After their marriage, Ralph Hamor became a land owner and a colonial official, much relied on by the English government and the Virginia Company. He later became Virginia Secretary of State. He and Elizabeth were listed in the census of 1624 in Jamestown. After only two years of marriage, Ralph Hamor died in 1626 at the age of 37. He left Elizabeth 200 acres of land on Hogs Island, an island which was primarily used to raise hogs which provided the much-sought-after pork that the population relied on.

I discovered a fascinating fact about Elizabeth's sojourn. After

Plymouth, Massachusetts was settled in 1620 by the Mayflower Puritans, Elizabeth visited that settlement. This fact was on a ship's manifest. Why, I wondered would she hazard a trip to another primitive settlement, far from Jamestown. I found the answer in searching the passengers of the Mayflower.

On that hazardous trip to Plymouth were two families with the last name of Fuller. The doctor aboard was Dr. Samuel Fuller with his wife and children. Also on board was Edward Fuller, the doctor's brother, with his wife and son. Many died on the trip from England and many died shortly after landing. Edward's wife died only a few days after disembarking from the Mayflower. Edward lived to sign the Mayflower Compact and then he died. Their young son, Samuel, was consequently raised by his uncle, Dr. Samuel Fuller. These Fuller settlers were Elizabeth's two uncles, brothers of her father. Edward was also my direct ancestor.

This begs another question: Was the Fuller family a Puritan family? Definitely, those on the Mayflower were Puritans. We know that their grandfather was imprisoned for defending Puritans, and we know that his son was also imprisoned. Does this imply that Elizabeth was a Puritan? She married as a teenager, so was she more influenced by her husband's beliefs? There is no record in Virginia of the Clements family practicing Puritanism. It remains a most interesting question.

Two years after the death of her second husband, Ralph Hamor in 1628, Elizabeth remarried once again to Captain Tobias Felgate, the master of the ship, "Supply". Sometime around this time, her son, Nicholas died. He would have only been around the age of 22. Another tragedy in her life. After her marriage to Captain Felgate, Elizabeth sailed with him to England which she seemed to have visited occasionally over the years. She died of unknown causes on August 26, 1633 in England. She was 53 years old.

In 1635, two years later, Thomas Felgate died in Virginia. Jeremiah was Elizabeth's heir, and her will showed that she left bequests for her daughter, Elizabeth, and Ezekial, her youngest son. Jeremiah inherited a plantation and the Hogs Island land, plus the interest in the ship.

Elizabeth had thrived economically and provided a legacy of courage and determination for her descendants.

Elizabeth's son, Jeremiah had inherited her plantation. He, in turn, was a tobacco planter. On the land he inherited, he built a Gothic Revival home called Claremont Manor. He, too, was able to travel on the family ship to England, but his home was Virginia where he had become a lawmaker of the colony. He married and had several children; only one survived to inherit the family estate – his daughter Elizabeth, named after his mother. Through this Clements line, one descendent was Samuel Longhorn Clements, Mark Twain. Another descendent was my grandmother, Henrietta Clements.

Elizabeth Ann Fuller lived through family turmoil and threat. She lived through plagues and lost her first husband, leaving her with three toddler sons and an infant daughter. She lived through dangerous crossings to Jamestown and lived in primitive conditions there. She survived unhealthy environments which eventually took the lives of two of her sons. She escaped Indian uprisings, and the death of a second husband. What would have destroyed one psychologically, emotionally and physically, she stayed strong enough to build a permanent home in a new world and left a lasting legacy for future generations. I am personally grateful.

Footnote: In 1699, the government and capital of Virginia was moved from Jamestown to Williamsburg, Virginia

ELIZABETH ANN FULLER

MARY ELLEN PLEASANT

―――――――

*"I know where I'm going, and I know the truth,
and I don't have to be what you want me to be.
I'm free to be what I want."*

―*Mohammad Ali*

―――――――

Mary Ellen Pleasant was not only wildly ahead of her time, she was ahead of *our* time. I had never heard of this fabulous woman until my good friend, Brad Geagley, started writing a book about her. Brad, a much-published author, Egyptian historian, researcher and professor, had read about Mary Ellen in Life Magazine in the 1970's, when that magazine devoted an entire issue to women's contributions to American history. Mary Ellen was prominently featured.

Brad felt compelled to research her life and write a book about this intriguing woman. He allows me to read what he writes before publication, and his opening chapters also intrigued and fascinated me. Brad never completed the draft of his book because he was informed that a white man writing about a black woman would never be published. He then shared his research with me when I asked permission to bring Mary Ellen Pleasant once again to life by presenting her in this endeavor.

Many newspaper and magazine writers tried to define this woman who refused to be categorized by anyone writing about her during her lifetime. Much misinformation and outright lies were written about her, but Mary Ellen fit no definitions of women of the Gilded Age, no expectations of mixed-race women, no understandings of bold, daring women in an age where women were subservient to men. She was unique and unconquerable. Look at the painting of her. This was a woman who was never defeated by birth, race, sex, education or the demands of a white, male-structured society.

We are very fortunate that in her 80's, as her life was drawing to a close, this woman who had refused to discuss her past or her present, decided that she must set the record straight. She started dictating the truth about her own history.

That autobiography was never completed, but it gives us glimpses into her childhood which shaped this indomitable woman. Self-taught, she was obviously highly intelligent. More importantly, she was an icon for women of color and a model for all women. Mary Ellen refused labels, refused stereotypical roles, demanded equality and most surprisingly for her time, demanded respect and dignity. She won it.

Mary Ellen was born free August 19, 1814 in Philadelphia, PA. at number 9 Barley Street. Her father was Alexander Louis Williams who was a pureblood Kanaka from Hawaii. Her mother, Claire Marie, was 16 years old when Mary Ellen was born. Claire Marie was a mixed-race woman of color from Louisiana. At that time, Philadelphia was where the Abolitionist Movement was born because it was dominated by Quakers who had formerly owned slaves, but later rejected that injustice and insisted on freedom of all men, black and white. Yet, Philadelphia was a strange and fearful place for people of color because, even though Philadelphia had outlawed slavery during revolutionary times, slave catchers were still allowed to stalk the streets to hunt for runaway slaves from the south. There was no one to verify that those people of color who lived in Philadelphia had not runaway to that city. All were in danger from these slave catchers whose income was derived from finding former slaves. Thus, black residents were both free and in danger of being enslaved.

Mary Ellen's father instilled fear in his daughter by warning her of these dangers; yet, he left her alone in their house as he traveled throughout New England. He was a successful importer of silks, satins and brocades from the Orient, who had to be on the road to sell and deliver his goods.

In her autobiography, she tells of her terror of being alone night after night. She was five to seven years old. Her mother, Claire Marie, was a live-in housekeeper in another home, and her child seldom ever saw her.

The only stable person in Mary Ellen's life was Delilah, a housekeeper who came every weekday morning to clean house. She was this child's only companion, and she loved Delilah dearly. Although Mary Ellen's father kept promising that he would sign her into school, he kept delaying, dashing her hopes that she could learn. Delilah, herself uneducated, knew the letters of the alphabet and some words from the Bible. She would pause in her work to teach those simple lessons to Mary Ellen. This child, only six and seven years old, started putting letters together in various ways and taught herself to read. This is how she described the process in her unfinished autobiography.

"I don't know when the letters began to arrange themselves into words, but soon they made sense to me. I had no great realization, and I cannot remember shouting out, "I can read. It just sort of all…. happened". One day I was illiterate, and the next I wasn't. It was the same way with numbers. I could add, subtract and multiply soon after I had learned to read. Even so, I still wanted the kind of education found in the school and waited patiently for my father to keep his promise."

As mentioned above, the most frightening and difficult part of Mary Ellen's life was being left alone in a house as Delilah had to leave to care for her own family. This little child of six describes her terror at being alone in a dark house at night.

"Alone in my attic room on the third floor, I heard the little wooden house creak and groan during the heat waves of July and August, when there wasn't a breath of wind to relieve us. And when the rainstorms came, oh my! Others might relish the coolness they brought, but the thunder and lightning seemed to want to tear our roof away! I cowered in my little bed, and heard the poor horses in the livery stable next door, shrieking and whinnying in terror – something I wanted to do too. I believed the winds were the howls of a terrible beast trying to claw its way through the shingles to spirit me away. It was only when Delilah arrived the next morning that I stopped shivering and emerged from under the covers."

Winters were easier for her because her father could not travel on muddy or snow-filled roads. However, by the time Mary Ellen was approaching her 7th year, she noticed many changes in him. He was drinking more and more and started selling anything of value in the house. Then he let Delilah go and asked if Mary Ellen would do the cooking and the housekeeping. She was thrilled to have him depend on her. She had a natural instinct for adding spices to enhance the flavors in her cooking and glowed in her father's praise.

Both her father and mother were tall, and Mary Ellen was unusually tall for her age and very strong as well. She cooked and cleaned and learned to do it all with her usual competency. She described how lonely she was, for her only encounters were with green grocers and fish mongers who set up their stalls on her street. She was a fierce bargainer and stated that she had to be. Her father gave her less and less money to buy food or run the household. He finally stopped working at all. A ship carrying all of her father's orders from Asia had been lost at sea, and he had used his credit to buy all the fabrics. He was now penniless and owed money to everyone for what he had ordered.

His solution: he sold his wife and daughter into work bondage to pay his debts. Once again, men owned their wives and daughters. Although in Philadelphia he could not sell them into slavery, he could sell them to work for others to pay off his debts. He sold her mother to a hotel to work for the rest of her life. Mary Ellen was seven years old, and he sold her into bondage until she reached the age of twenty-two. When a policeman and the owner of the house they were in came to evict them, her father held her and in words she never forgot said this:

"You go with these men now. All little girls have to grow up sometime, and you just have to do it a little sooner than most. You're going to go to work in a house, just like your mama does. Aren't you the finest housekeeper in Philadelphia already? Haven't you been making yourself ready for just this day? You're not to worry, for I'll come for you just as soon as I can. Then you, your mama and I, we'll all live somewhere else …. New York, maybe. And as for schooling, I've given that landlord of ours all the cash I had on hand, enough to send you to school. Why, when I see you next, you'll be an educated lady!"

Mary Ellen then wrote, "I looked into his brown eyes and knew that everything he said was a lie. But I nodded my head. What was the use of fighting the inescapable? I packed my few duds in a cardboard box; my father tied it up with twine and we went downstairs. "Now kiss me bye" he said. I averted my head when he brought his lips close. I drew back, thinking – this must be how Jesus felt when Judas kissed him. It was the last time I ever saw him."

The Quaker landlord took me with him. When the child asked if her father had really left money for her schooling, he told her that it was he who had paid her father for her indenture and for the indenture of her mother. He told her that the $267.38 that her father owed him was paid with her being sold as a servant on Nantucket Island for twelve years.

"I felt my young heart grow cold. Seven years old is too young an age to learn that even your nearest and dearest can betray you. I made a vow that it would be the last time any man would buy or sell me. And I made up my mind, too, that no matter where Nantucket was – I was going to prosper there."

Mary Ellen was to spend the next sixteen years of her life in Nantucket. Although she was in bondage, she was fortunate to be bonded to an older Quaker woman who ran a general store, Hussey's Mercantile, and whose home was above that store. Mrs. Hussey owned and ran her store and already had two other girls who were hired, not bonded, working there. There was ample work for the three girls and their kindly employer. Quakers were abolitionists and did not believe in slavery but apparently did not see the incongruity in paying for bonded workers. Mrs. Hussey was a particularly kindly soul who insisted that she be called "Grandma". She gave Mary Ellen the warmest bedroom in the house and always worried about her health and well- being. In fact, Grandma always treated her like a granddaughter

The first job for the newcomer was the easiest ones in this household/ store. Cleanliness was of paramount importance to Grandma, so each morning the house was swept and polished. When the breakfast dishes were done, Mary Ellen took the cow to the fields. Her big chore was to do the laundry every day except Sunday. Lye soap was used to launder clothes, and it was caustic and could burn the hands of the laundress. However, Grandma sent for the newest device for washing clothes – a tub with a special paddle which could be twisted back and forth. Thus, Mary Ellen never had her hands in the soapy, scalding water. When the clothes were clean, she hung them on clothes lines in back of the store.

Much later in her life, she owned a number of laundries which brought in considerable income. She made certain that she always bought the latest innovations to not only help her employees, but to greatly increase her profits. She credited her success in these endeavors directly to Grandma Hussey.

Mary Ellen learned another valuable lesson in Nantucket. In her words:

"Nantucket truly was an island of independent women. Because their husbands were at sea for two and three years at a time, it was left to them to rule and provide for their families. When the men returned, weary from their whaling work, they cheerfully gave their praise to their wives and let them be. I would see these same men on Union Street following meekly behind their women, humble and silent, while the wives frequently stopped to "get the news" from their female friends. Though the menfolk were left to stand behind them, bored and fidgeting, they didn't dare say a thing. I'm sure these same husbands and wives loved each other, but I can also imagine that the men were as anxious to get away once the whaling season began, as the women were to see them gone, for it was women's rules and women's governance on that island. Over the years, I began to think theirs was a perfect arrangement for a successful marriage, with husband and wife spending four or five months together during the winter months, followed by one or two years apart. There was a song I learned to sing called the Nantucket girl's song…"

Then I'll haste to wed a sailor and send him off to sea
For a life of independence is the pleasant life for me.
And when he says "Goodbye, my love, I'm off across the sea
First, I cry for his departure, then I laugh because I'm free

Another gift from her Nantucket life was the enhancement of her cooking skills. Grandma Hussey did not like to cook and was not good at it, but she was reluctant to allow Mary Ellen to take over that responsibility because she feared she was too young and would burn or scald herself. However, the girl demonstrated that she had mastered all the skills necessary and was a gifted cook who took Grandma's recipes and added the extra zest which made a meal extraordinary.

From then on, Mary Ellen prepared all the meals in their home which she loved to do. Many years later, she also owned and operated very successful restaurants in San Francisco which also enhanced the fortune she accumulated. The one fly in the ointment of her early years was the presence of one of the other hired girls who lived and worked in Grandma Hussey's emporium.

This girl, Purity, who was older than the rest, was cruel, a thief, a bully and a liar. She was a poor girl that Grandma had hired because her family was so poor. Purity was mean to the other hired girl as well, but she was particularly cruel to Mary Ellen whom she called pickaninny and constantly pinched and hit. Although Purity never acted out her hatred and spite when Grandma was there, she constantly made life miserable for the other two girls who never told on her.

After a few years of torment, Mary Ellen concocted a scheme which trapped the unsuspecting Purity in a seeming theft. Purity raged and accused Mary Ellen of the mischief, but the evidence was conclusive that she was the culprit. Grandma sent her away, and years later, Mary Ellen wrote this: "Looking back, I owe it to Purity for letting me discover the truth of my character – that I was as brave as a gaming rooster, always ready for a fight when it sees one coming. I'd rather be a corpse than a coward. I've always said that it was Purity who taught me how to fight to win. I learned how soothing to the soul it was to see justice done. I learned how good it felt to humble a hated enemy. Finally, I learned that – no matter the odds – I would always be able to take care of myself. Justice brought Purity low, but the vengeance was mine, and it pleased me greatly. No one ever tried to make me into a victim again – well, excepting one man. But I made his life such a misery that it cost him dear."

Life was now good for Mary Ellen. Grandma believed that children needed fresh air and after dinner each day, she sent them out to play. Mary Ellen enjoyed running races with the boys and played primarily with them, as the other mothers considered her too wild for a girl. As she grew older, Mary Ellen blossomed in Nantucket growing to her full height, over 6 ft. tall. She was highly intelligent, very pretty and quick to learn how to manage a store and entice new customers to shop. She also became a skilled dress maker and made all her own clothes. She soon started making shawls and gloves to sell in the store. Grandma paid her for these items, and she saved all her money toward buying herself out of her bond.

One other, very important, circumstance changed for Mary Ellen. After Purity's welcomed departure, Grandma Hussey sent for a young "modern Quaker" to work in the store. Her name was Phoebe, and she quickly became the first real friend that Mary Ellen ever made. Phoebe was well educated, and she soon sent for her old school books and started teaching Mary Ellen in the evenings. They studied together as their friendship blossomed.

Mary Ellen was not eighteen years old. Interestingly, in her auto-biography, Mary Ellen revealed that she had discovered something very important. "I had always studied the people who came into Grandma's shop. If you do that every day, like I did, you soon became a master at reading all their signs – will they buy, or will they just look? Have they got much money to spend, or very little? It got so I could always tell. The truth was that I really didn't have much need for more book education. I met people in that shop who had studied every book in the library, yet they were lost to the world. They really knew nothing about it or the people who inhabited it. I found that you must either study books or human nature, slighting one for the other. I have seen many people who talk all day but never talk a minute's worth of sense. Yet when I have anything to say – people listen. They never go to sleep on me. After everything was said and done – I suppose that I got the education I truly needed in Nantucket, if not the one I had always wanted."

Phoebe was also instrumental in freeing Mary Ellen from another expectation. The Quaker Church was a part of her life since her arrival at age seven. Grandma Hussey took her to services every Sunday and taught the religion's philosophy on a daily basis. It was a religion that opposed slavery, urged honesty and kindness and applauded hard work. What Mary Ellen particularly liked was the fact that women were encouraged to speak their minds when "the spirit moved them" and not sit in silence while the men did all the talking.

Phoebe was a Quaker, but a much more liberal one. She recognized that Mary Ellen needed to be exposed to more people of color and their belief systems. When the new African Baptist Church opened its doors, Phoebe talked to her Aunt Mary who agreed to let Mary Ellen attend the new church. She also gave her a dime for the collection plate. Grandma explained that she was hopeful that this beloved young woman would become a Quaker, but that she had to find her own path to God. "Thee are a good girl, Mary Ellen, and I know thee will find Him wherever you worship."

Mary Ellen gave credit to this religion in these words… "The Quakers are like that, tolerant and kind, never forcing you to believes in this or that. I have always respected them for their broad-mindedness and have sometimes even told people over the years that I was a "Friend."

As she writes later, Mary Ellen attended churches of many faiths – Quaker, Baptist, Catholic and many other protestant churches. She felt that all served a higher good and was comfortable wherever she attended. However, her first visit to the African Baptist Church was life-changing. Unlike the quiet Quaker meetings, there was high emotion and much vocal shouting and cheering. The sermon had been a passionate renunciation of slavery, and Mary Ellen was enraptured and thrilled. She described the impact of that powerful sermon thus: "At that moment I knew Nantucket had given me its final gift – my life's passion. Commerce may have been my vocation, to be sure, but the Abolition of Slavery, which I first learned at the African Baptist, became my avocation. ..... I wanted to work for a cause that was greater than me." From that moment, she considered that she was reborn.

For years, she had been saving to buy back her bond and had accumulated $30.00, a great sum in those days. She immediately returned to the church and gave every cent to the Reverend to continue his work of abolishing slavery. As she said later, she learned that day to give money away when it was for a worthy cause. It was a habit that she continued for a lifetime. Not only did she continue to attend church services but also attended political meetings almost nightly.

At church and political gatherings, Mary Ellen kept noticing a man much older than she, who was much deferred to by the minister and other notable men. His name was James William Smith, the much-respected captain of a ship. He was to become her first husband.

One night as she was going home after a political meeting, she smelled smoke and saw the glow of a fire. As she ran forward, she realized that it was Grandma's store and home that was burning. Stored oil was exploding and the fire raged throughout the building. Grandma lay prone on the street in front of her store. Phoebe sat next to her, holding her head in her lap. Both girls had noticed that this beloved woman had been becoming more forgetful as she aged.

Apparently, she had let a candle burn, and it ignited the fire. The shock of the loss of everything she had worked for – home and business, was too much. Grandma died of a heart attack on the street as the fire raged on.

Both girls cried throughout the night. A kindly Quaker woman took them home at dawn to stay with her until Phoebe's parents, the Gardiners, arrived. A few days later, Phoebe was married to the ship captain she had been engaged to. Mary Ellen was her maid of honor. She realized Grandma's death freed her of the hated bond; but she had no idea what to do with that freedom. She did realize that life in Nantucket had come to a permanent close.

Mary Ellen had given all her money to the Baptist church. She searched through the charred ruins of the store and found twenty bottles of wine which she sold for $1.00 each. With her $20.00, she journeyed with the Gardiners to Boston, Massachusetts to start her new life. It was 1836, and she was 22 years old.

Phoebe and her new husband, Edward, insisted that Mary Ellen live with them rent-free. She initially wanted to be their housekeeper to earn her way, but Edward already had plenty of servants. Phoebe made it amply clear that Mary Ellen was her cherished "sister" and was a guest, not a servant. The young couple were friends with all the prominent abolitionists in the area and entertained them frequently.

For this young woman of color meeting all these people, abolition soon became the central issue of her life. It was among this group of people that Mary Ellen first encountered John Brown. She stated that "John Brown was the first person in the abolitionist movement who finally made sense to me." He made sense because most of the abolitionists were people with words and prayers, hoping to persuade the slavers to change their minds. John Brown was a man of action willing to resort to even violent measures to end slavery. Mary Ellen favored his views.

From the time she moved in with her "sister", Phoebe, Mary Ellen looked for work doing those tasks in which she was proficient. She had a huge collection of recipes – first gathered from Grandma, then from all the women she met in Boston – all enhanced by her own spices and herbs. Still, she was unable to find work as a cook in any household.

Because the law in Massachusetts stated that if a slave stayed more than ninety days in the state, they were to be declared free, the southerners sent their slave cooks back to the south just before the end of three months. They then had them returned a week later with new supplies from the South. Transplanted southerners only wanted their own "mammies" to do the cooking.

Mary Ellen also knew well how to work in a shop – how to run it and how to make it financially successful – but no shop owner would hire her. Her last great talent was sewing, and she finally found work in a men's haberdashery. She made a dollar a week. The two brothers who owned the store were the first Jews she ever encountered. She grew to enjoy working for them because "they weren't tainted by the scorn that most Americans showed to dark-skinned people or to other foreigners." She found that "people from foreign lands were usually quick to see past my color to a real person beneath." Her description went further: "This wasn't true of my own countrymen. Far from it – our entire country seemed poisoned by race."

The Kaminsky brothers owned the haberdashery and had fled Poland when the Cossacks destroyed their entire village. They had survived by hiding all night in a well, shivering in the cold water. They first escaped to Germany, then were sent to America to work on farms in Texas. However, when the ship stopped in Boston, they had slipped overboard to find work as tailors, their chosen profession. After three years, they had saved enough to open their own shop. They understood prejudice, suffering and racism; so, they treated Mary Ellen well and she enjoyed working for them. All three of them still lived in fear of having to flee the intolerance and hatred aimed at them. Mary Ellen wrote thus, "Violence seemed always to lurk beneath the surface in America, directed at immigrants like the Kaminsky brothers, or at dark people like me."

In Boston, Mary Ellen, saw the great divide among those who supported the abolishment of slavery and those who supported slavery because they relied on it economically. She was witness to a mob who wanted to kill a publisher friend because he wrote of the hypocrisy. It was in Boston also that she once again came into contact with Mr. Smith, owner of a mill and brickyard and a successful building contractor. When he asked her to marry him, she found out that he was also of mixed race and had let people assume he was white because it made it easier to advance in business.

Mary Ellen was initially concerned that Mr. Smith was twice her age and had two sons and a daughter by his first marriage. Mr. Smith insisted that she convert to Catholicism, which she did. They were married at the Holy Cross Church. She wore a beautiful wedding gown that the Kaminsky brothers had lovingly and lavishly handmade for her. The reception was at Phoebe and Edward's home. Mary Ellen then moved to the beautiful home of her new husband, James Henry Smith. She gave birth there to her only child, Elizabeth (Lizzie) Smith.

Sometime after 1848, James Smith died leaving Mary Ellen with a substantial legacy. James Smith's home and businesses would have been inherited by his son from his first marriage, but he also left Mary Ellen a substantial legacy. She now had independence and money.

Within the next year or so, Mary Ellen met and married a former slave, John James Pleasant. It was then that Mary Ellen and her new husband made the decision to follow her many abolitionist friends to San Francisco. They took passage on a ship which had to stop in New Orleans because of weather. Passengers stayed in New Orleans for two months or so. It was there that later slanderous writers said she studied voodoo under a priestess there. Many scandal sheets ever after called her a "Voodoo Queen" who practiced all sorts of evil things in the basement of her home.

However, the truth was that the Pleasants sailed on to San Francisco, where Mary Ellen immediately went to work as housekeeper/cook/hostess to many of the wealthiest and most powerful men in that city. Even though she had brought the $15,000 legacy with her which was a fortune at that time, she believed in work.

She also used her exceptional listening skills in those homes to learn about how to invest and grow her money. She learned well.

It was obvious that Mary Ellen was the dominant money maker and force in her marriage. Although her fame and reputation grew, little was ever said about her husband who didn't die until 1877. Mary Ellen intuitively understood the benefits of investment, and she speculated in the stock and money markets with great success. As her wealth grew, so did her fame in that city. Unfortunately, along with wealth and fame came jealousy, resentment and many myths and stories, most of which were outright lies. What was true was she invested in laundries, restaurants and high-end boarding houses. All of these were highly successful because she had knowledge gleaned from her childhood and girlhood when living with Grandma Hussey.

She also had a genius for making money through financial speculation and her specialized training of all the staff who worked for her in her many businesses. During that time, she personally paid for fugitive slaves and freedmen to flee to San Francisco. She then housed, fed and trained those former slaves for jobs in the homes of the wealthy and influential in San Francisco. That staff then reported to her all the financial and personal information they gleaned. She never revealed that information to anyone but used those secrets of others to advance her own fortune and ambition.

During this time, she was both widely admired and widely disliked. Those who admired her were not only impressed by her business acumen and ability to create successful businesses, but they were astounded by her generosity and kindness in giving money away to worthy causes and individuals. She gained more pleasure from giving money away than from accumulating it.

She helped to found and then was very active financially and personally in the Underground Railroad which was bringing runaway slaves to San Francisco. She was much beloved by the oppressed and those runaway slaves whom she fed and housed until she could find them employment or could aid them in starting their own businesses. In one book about Mary Ellen Pleasant, the writer, Lerone Bennett, Jr. described her abolitionist activities as well as describing her as a "one-woman social agency". He described another of her philanthropic activities as follows: "She was engaged on another front, defending and advancing the cause of unprotected females, Black and White. This was a hard and unforgiving age for unprotected females, and San Francisco was the hardest and most unforgiving haven of all. The woman who fell unsuspectingly into the clutches of operators of whorehouses and dives, the girl who miscalculated and got pregnant, the pretty and weak-willed widow left with no means of support: for all these, for the tempted, the weak-willed, the unlucky, Mary Ellen Pleasant was a haven and a lighthouse."

On some occasions, the record shows, she stormed into dives and physically rescued attractive young arrivals. On other occasions, she found homes for unwanted babies. At the same time, she was hiding fugitive slaves in her homes and in the homes of the wealthy and influential. She also paid for legal services for all those she was rescuing."

In addition, because she had her trained servants in the homes of the most powerful, she knew many secrets which she never revealed. She did use that knowledge to force many wealthy men to support their illegitimate children. One admirer called her "the Mother of Civil Rights in California".

In 1858, Mary Ellen, who was 44 years old and a millionairess, abruptly leased her businesses and went to Canada to further support John Brown, who was now famous for his exploits of freeing enslaved people and training them to fight for the freedom of other slaves. He was hated and feared in the South and was a hero to the Abolitionists. In Canada, Mary Ellen brought Brown a substantial amount of money for his planned strike in Harper's Ferry and spent much time planning with him. After he was captured and hanged for treason and insurrection, she returned to San Francisco. She maintained until her dying day that it was the most important and significant act of her life. At her insistence the carving on her headstone at the cemetery read only, "SHE WAS A FRIEND OF JOHN BROWN".

In 1955, Rosa Parks refused to give up her bus seat to a white person. She was ejected but Martin Luther King took up her cause and started a bus boycott. This all led to the Civil Rights Movement. In 1866, eighty-nine years before that famous event, Mary Ellen Pleasant staged a sit-in on a San Francisco streetcar because the driver tried to evict her. She sued the Omnibus Railroad Company and won. The company made public the following statement, "Negroes would hereafter be allowed to ride on the car, let the effect on the Company's business be what it might."

In fact, Mary Ellen sued many companies and individuals for racist behaviors and policies. She won the majority of those lawsuits. During all this, she was the major force in fundraising efforts for many causes and institutions, including the Black Masonic Lodge, the Black Baptist, the AM and the AME Zion churches. She was quoted, "I am a Catholic, but one church was the same as another to me. It was all for the cause."

Over the years, publications and scandal sheets starting calling this powerful woman, "Mammy Pleasant". She hated this title and refused to respond to anyone who used that racist title, "Mammy". She made certain that San Francisco would know of her charities and her social agenda. In 1865 Mary Ellen proudly sponsored an elaborate and fashionable wedding for her daughter at the AME Zion Church in San Francisco.

It was also around this time, that she met Thomas Bell, a Scotsman stockbroker. There was always, then and now, much speculation about their true relationship; but this much we know is true. They were business partners and more. Mary Ellen had built a San Francisco mansion; she was the owner. He moved into that mansion with a young wife that some said was one of the girls that Mary Ellen rescued from a whorehouse.

He and his wife, Teresa Percy, had several children while living there. However, it was Mary Ellen who ran the house, handled the finances of everyone and made all the important decisions. When Mary Ellen went out of the house, she wore the clothes of a highly placed servant – black, well-designed dresses with a white apron. However, when she was in her home and entertaining there, she wore richly appointed, fashionable clothes of the time. Mary Ellen and Thomas Bell described themselves as "rare, warm personal friends". Many in San Francisco insisted that they were lovers, but the truth in their close friendship was never revealed. Rumor and speculation may have been widespread, but it always remained only gossip.

Thomas Bell's wife, Teresa Percy, hated Mary Ellen who had wielded all of the power in the house they shared. Although it was widely accepted that Teresa Percy was mentally unstable or disturbed, her bizarre accusations against her old nemesis were accepted by many racists and others who hated Mary Ellen's wealth, influence and power. Teresa accused her of acts of voodoo, of torture, of violence against children – all purported to have taken place in the basement of the house they shared. These wild accusations were widely published and believed by some; however, police interviewed many servants who had worked in that house over the years. They all denied that any such thing had ever happened, for they had lived in that house and knew all that was going on there.

In 1899, Teresa relied on the laws of the time which allowed the widow of the man who had lived in the house to dispose of the property at her will. Even though the house was in the name of Mary Ellen Pleasant and all the belongings were hers, this 85-year-old woman was forced to depart and move to a six-room apartment. She still owned a great deal of property, but her liquid assets were tied up in her joint business with Tom Bell, so she had to move. Ever the fighter, she sued, charging that she was a victim of a legal conspiracy. She included in her suit that the property, including the fortune in diamonds claimed by Teresa Bell was actually hers. As all this dragged through the courts, Mary Ellen lived in the cramped quarters which were uncomfortable and cold. During this time, she had a visitor who offered her a small fortune to reveal the secrets of San Francisco society. She dismissed him, saying: "I have never needed money bad enough to betray anyone."

Interestingly, although Teresa Bell continued to fabricate scurrilous lies about the woman she so hated, Teresa's children abandoned their mother and rallied around Mary Ellen in her sparse apartment. They visited and did caretaking duties until she died. During the last few years of her life, much was stolen by others from that apartment, including papers, jewelry and other valuables.

One interviewer who came to the apartment was afraid of her infamous anger, but she answered thus: "Me? Mad? I used to get mad, but no more. I used to waste a powerful lot of energy in that way, but it's foolish. When you have eighty-seven years over your head and the experience I've had, you recognize the fact that other folks have the right to their point of view. If you think the same as I do, then there's no disruption and no fight. I like to fight, and I'm as brave as a rooster – a gaming rooster – ready for the fight if I see one coming. I'd rather be a corpse than a coward. If I'm dead, I'm all right; but as long as I live, I want to fight to win. And I don't want to be carried to victory on beds of ease, either. I like to go through bloody scenes. The papers can say what they want, as far as I'm concerned. When I am in a fight, any byplay doesn't faze me. Some folks take themselves too seriously. I take life as a joke and get lots of fun out of it. I know on which side my bread is buttered, and if it ain't buttered at all, I eat it just the same. You tell those newspaper people that they may be smart, but I'm smarter. They deal with words. Some folks say that words were made to reveal thought. That ain't so. Words were made to conceal thought."

She went on to tell this reporter: "I haven't much book education. I study people. I don't require much book education, because I don't need it. I don't deal with books. I know people who study books until they know all the books in the library, but when they meet people, their knowledge is locked in the library, and they're lost out in the world. I'm a great believer in work; do your work and get through with it."

What Mary Ellen was most adamant about, however, was this: "I don't like to be called Mammy by everybody. Put that down. I am not Mammy to everybody in California. Between you and me, I don't care anything about it, but they shan't do it – they shan't nickname me at my age. It just rouses my Kanaka blood." To the end, this incredible woman was willing to take on the world in defense of her dignity and her place in an openly racist country.

"You either take what has been dealt to you and allow it to make you a better person, or you allow it to tear you down."… John Shipp

Mary Ellen Pleasant never allowed anything to tear her down. Her health was fading rapidly during these last years in that apartment, and she received cards, letters and flowers from those from her past who were still living. A white friend of Mary Ellen's found her delirious and alone and had her moved to her own home. Mary Ellen Pleasant was 90 years old at this time, and she died two months later on January 11, 1904.

It has been difficult for those interested in her to sort out the many stories of her birth, childhood, early years and adulthood. Ebony Magazine, a popular Black magazine, attempted to sort out the myths, lies and half-truths in an article which defended her. I have borrowed much information from that article in this chapter. What was difficult for all to comprehend was that Mary Ellen told different stories about her past to different listeners. She was quite open about the fact that she did not care what others thought and found it amusing to startle them with fabricated information.

What I have chosen to highlight in this article is what she revealed to a trusted friend who was writing her autobiography prior to her death. She stated that she wanted to set the record straight and tell the real story. Although this autobiography was never finished, I have selected some of the stories which Mary Ellen told to her trusted friend, for I believe these are the real truths of her past and her exemplary life.

Mary Ellen Pleasant was remarkable in every way – in the life she lived, in the published accounts of her life and, most importantly, in her actions. She lived a life of honesty, integrity, compassion, generosity and action. She was an integral part of the anti-slavery movement, both financially and personally in her active role in the Underground Railroad for slaves. If suspected, she would have been imprisoned and killed. Yet, she was tireless and fearless.

Mary Ellen was also a brilliant business woman, amassing a fortune and becoming the first black woman millionaire in the United States. All of her endeavors and successes occurred during the time of slavery. So, she had to daily overcome prejudice, racism, sexism, lack of education and jealousy of her incredible success.

In a world designed to defeat her talents, she won. She won in business; she won in helping to free her fellow man; she won dignity and respect. Finally, she won my heart and the hearts of all the women whose opportunities opened up because she led the way and showed the world the true meaning of courage.

"Where there is no struggle, there is no strength."
—*Oprah Winfrey*

MARY ELLEN PLEASANT

ZADDIE BUNKER

"When you are actually powerful, you don't need to be petty."

—*Jon Stewart*

The last 125 years have been significant in terms of improvements in the treatment and the status of women. Zaddie Bunker helped to lead the way during those years. Once again, she was before her time in her thinking and her actions. During her lifetime, time and again she dared many new things, and she won admiration and respect for her deeds and actions. She was, indeed, before her time.

Although I have lived my retirement years in the Palm Springs area, I had never heard of Zaddie Bunker who had been well known in this area before her death in 1969. I was making a presentation to the Women's Entrepreneurial Group of Palm Springs, and my book was discussed. A member of the Entrepreneurial Group, Kathleen Strukoff, suggested that I research Zaddie for inclusion in my book. I followed this excellent advice, and here is the chapter on another remarkable woman, Zaddie Bunker.

ZADDIE DAWSON was born August 29, 1887 in Carroll, Reynolds, Missouri. Her parents were Elija Dawson, born in Missouri in 1851 and her mother, Sarah Frances Romine, was born in Missouri in 1857. Zaddie claimed in records of the time that she had only completed the 8th grade in Missouri. According to an article by Renee Brown of the Palm Springs Historical Society in the Desert Sun newspaper, she was teaching school in Missouri when she met and married Chauncey Edward Bunker, a blacksmith who had been born in 1884. The Historical Society of Palm Springs also had records stating that Zaddie had been teaching grade school in Missouri, even though she had only completed 8th grade herself. Apparently, it was legal in the early 1900's to teach school without formal education or training.

Ed Bunker had partly grown up in California. He had come to Missouri to work for an uncle who had a lumber company. However, he had always wanted to return to California. After he wed Zaddie, they had a child, Frances Ann Bunker, born in 1907. In 1914, when Frances was seven years old, Ed and Zaddie packed everything in an old, converted two-cylinder Maxwell car and started their trip to California. There were few cars at that time and fewer mechanics. Ed, who loved cars, learned to be a mechanic so that he could repair their car on the long trip. He bought the necessary tools to keep the car going and the tires repaired. At that time, most of the roads were still dirt, so it was a slow and bumpy journey.

Ed entered into a partnership with two other men to rent 1,000 acres in San Jacinto and plant potatoes. The potatoes were harvested and stored in a warehouse for spring sale. Unfortunately, the huge freeze in the winter ruined all the potatoes. Ed and Zaddie were broke.

It was Ed's idea to move to the unincorporated and sparsely settled desert area of Palm Springs. He borrowed money from a sister for the move and started working toward his dream of opening a car garage. Initially, Ed worked for a building contractor for 25 cents an hour, and Addie was earning 25 cents an hour sewing and making clothes for others. During that time, they learned that a paved highway running past Palm Springs was to be built from Banning to Indio. Banning and Indio had automobile garages, and they realized that Palm Springs would need a repair garage. Zaddie knew nothing about car repair, and Ed had only worked on his own car, so they both took an auto repair correspondence course called Van Dyke's Automobile Engineering. They also studied the manuals of the different car models then in use.

When this young family arrived in Palm Springs, there were only

25 white people living in the area. The majority of the inhabitants were Native Americans belonging to the Cahuilla Tribe. In 1916, one of Zaddie's sisters let them borrow money, and they leased land and built a tent-house to live in. The young family lived in the tent house for two years. During that time, they used the money that Ed made as a blacksmith and Zaddie made as a seamstress to install hardwood floors, wood walls and a canvas roof onto the tent. They were also slowly building their corrugated metal garage during those two years, and they finally opened Bunker's Garage in 1916.

In 1916, there were only four cars in Palm Springs, one of which was theirs. Fortunately for them, 1916 was also the year that the paved road was completed, so their business started flourishing. They bought additional tools to respond to the many different problems that these early cars experienced. They were still not making enough to cover their expenses, so Ed worked for 25 cents an hour building fences, digging ditches and other chores for a builder. Zaddie went to work as the mechanic in the garage. She was a quick learner and soon was an excellent mechanic.

Zaddie and Ed, ever the entrepreneurs, recognized that Palm Springs, California was so attractive for visitors because of its balmy winters; and they wanted to make money to invest in land and more businesses. At that time, most people came to Palm Springs area for their health, so the warm winter climate was attracting more people to the area.

World War I started in 1914, and the man who had been driving guests back and forth between the railroad station, the hotel and local homes in Palm Springs left to serve overseas. At that time, anyone who purchased a car could drive that car without a license, but the state of California made it a law that anyone driving a car for "hire" had to have a license. In order to obtain a license, one had to simply send a $2.00 fee to Sacramento. Zaddie had obtained a 7-passenger Benham car which had the luxury of Westinghouse air-springs on it. She was the first woman in California to have a chauffeur's license, and she transported tourists and goods from the train station into Palm Springs. She also drove visitors to the canyons to see the sights. She had to drive in sand which was very tricky. Most drivers stalled, but Zaddie learned how to get her passengers back and forth safely.

Between those trips, she still ran and operated Bunker's Garage. She charged $1.00 an hour for repair work. With her additional chauffeur's income, she and Ed started purchasing parcel after parcel of land on the main street of Palm Springs (now Palm Canyon Drive). That paved road was then designated by the state as a highway.

Luck was with them when one of the Hollywood studios wanted to make a Western film in this area. Ed and Zaddie leased the land adjacent to their garage, and the studio built a set that included small houses with piped-in water.

Zaddie talked her sister, Lillie Goff, into coming to Palm Springs to help her cook for the movie crew. The two sisters accepted any job the film makers offered. They sewed, ironed and cleaned; anything to earn more money. Zaddie also hauled freight for the studios and even appeared as an extra when needed. After filming was finished, the studio abandoned those small buildings. Since these structures were on their land, the Bunkers used them for rentals. Zaddie opened the first Studebaker dealership in Palm Springs in one of those buildings.

Zaddie was the oldest daughter in her family, and she was so enthusiastic about living in the California desert and the financial possibilities there, that she convinced her parents, Sarah and Elijah, to move there. Elijah bought a piece of land, purchased five cows and sold milk to the townspeople for 20 cents a quart. Zaddie's two younger sisters, Lillie and Henrietta, also came to live nearby, and both of them also worked hard to save money to invest in real estate. Henrietta and her husband, Ellis Parker, eventually built a 38-room hotel which also thrived. Henrietta and Zaddie together bought a lot across the street from Bunker's Garage. That lot eventually became a part of the Desert Fashion Plaza.

Zaddie had helped her family become prosperous land and real estate owners. Zaddie's husband, Ed, also brought his family to Palm Springs where he helped them get established. These two pioneers lived in Palm Springs for ten years before electricity was installed, and they were two of the leading citizens who pushed for this innovation. Since Ed and Zaddie were major owners of property along the highway through Palm Springs, they and the other owners paid for the first sewer line on Palm Canyon Drive. They had become leading and influential members of the community.

According to the Desert Sun newspaper article, Frances Ann, Zaddie's daughter, had studied to become an osteopathic physician and surgeon. In 1929, at the age of 22 years, she graduated with that degree and returned to Palm Springs to open up her practice in an office in one of her parent's buildings in downtown Palm Springs. She soon met Earle Strebe, a movie projectionist who worked at The Desert Inn and the Oasis Hotel. In 1930, Frances and Earle were married. Frances soon gave up her practice in order to spend more time with her new and very busy husband.

After Frances left home to be married, Ed divorced Zaddie in order to marry a younger woman. During Ed and Zaddie's marriage, the two had purchased a sizeable amount of real estate both in Palm Springs and in the mountains near Idyllwild. In the divorce, Zaddie was awarded all of the real estate in Palm Springs and a large portion of the land in the mountains. Years later, Zaddie laughed about the divorce saying that Ed had traded her in for a new model, but she was the one who ended up with the best part of the trade because she was the one that ended up becoming a millionaire.

Ed and his new wife settled on the remaining part of the mountain property which he was awarded after the divorce and opened a cattle ranch which he called Bunker Ranch. Ed operated this ranch until his death in 1969. Zaddie never remarried. She had become a skilled mechanic and stayed in Palm Springs and ran the garage alone. She never ceased buying land and investing in property.

Zaddie had always been intrigued with airplanes and wanted to learn to fly, but Ed had discouraged her. After the divorce, she took flying lessons, soloed in 1952 and obtained her pilot's license when she was 60 years old. She received her multi-engine rating at age 63. She then bought her own plane which she called "Zaddie's Rocking Chair". She had that name stenciled on her plane's fuselage. Her adventurous spirit kept her challenging herself. At the age of 71 she passed the tough physical tests demanded of Air Force jet pilots. She then requested and was granted permission to fly an Air Force F100 Super Saber jet and was one of the first women to break the sound barrier.

By this time, Zaddie had become famous and was known widely as "the flying grandmother", later "the flying great-grandmother". She not only won the Powder Puff Derby air race, but she also beat five male pilots when she won an airplane race from Dateland, Arizona to El Centro, California. Zaddie was widely admired for her indomitable spirit, and the press who loved her, regularly reported on all of her exploits. Because of this renown, she was invited to Edwards Air Force Base to be installed as an honorary lieutenant-colonel in the U.S. Air Force. This was a very great honor, and Zaddie was a very proud recipient of that title.

In 1959, the "Supersonic Great-Grandmother" went to Spain as part of President Dwight D. Eisenhower's People to People program. According to The Desert Sun, she "stole the hearts of city officials and 80 little orphan girls in Seville."

Another time, Zaddie went to Washington D.C. for an air race. When she returned to her hotel, she learned that then Vice-President Richard Nixon's secretary had been calling all afternoon. This former desert mechanic was invited to meet Vice-President (later President) Nixon who was an admirer of this amazing woman.

Also, in 1959 there was a popular television show called "This Is Your Life" hosted by the well-known host, Ralph Edwards. Millions of people watched this show as each week a celebrity or well-known person was surprised with the story of their life. On February 23 of that year, Zaddie had been told to attend an aeronautical aviation meeting in Burbank. As she stepped out of her plane onto the tarmac, Ralph Edwards strode up and said, "Zaddie Bunker, "This is Your Life!"

Age never slowed down the adventurous Zaddie, who loved to ride her horse up into the canyons and into the mountains when she was home. However, her private plane and her love for adventure kept her traveling widely. At age 79, she applied for astronaut duty but was turned down, no doubt because of her age. The U.S. Air Force did, however, give her a passing grade on her physical which she had taken to ready herself for an Apollo moon flight. Because she was an honorary lieutenant-colonel in the U.S. Air Force and had passed a tough physical, they invited her to spend some time in the space capsule simulator. She was not in the least daunted by the experience of being weightless and floating about in a capsule while performing demanding tasks. She was disappointed that she didn't get the opportunity to go to the moon, and she stated to everyone that she could have done it. Everyone agreed.

The daring, fearless Zaddie became well known during her lifetime. What is unknown to many is her ability as a business woman. With a self-proclaimed 8th grade education, a mechanics license, a willingness to do any kind of menial work to get ahead and an obviously brilliant mind for investment and business, Zaddie became a leading citizen in Palm Springs and brought renown to her city, her state and her country. These are just a few of her commercial successes.

Her daughter, Frances, had married Earle Strebe who became a partner with Zaddie in much of her investment and development plans. Earl came to Palm Springs in 1927 and worked as a bellman at the Desert Inn Hotel. He was asked to show guests movies and soon became known as an excellent movie projectionist. His mother-in-law, Zaddie, invested in his dream of opening two movie theatres (one of which is the famous Plaza Theatre in downtown Palm Springs.) As those two theatres flourished, he and Zaddie continued to invest widely in real estate, both buying and leasing their properties all over town. Ed eventually was president of the Chamber of Commerce and was a member of the Palm Springs City Council. Zaddie Bunker became one of the wealthiest women in the city. As her wealth and renown grew, Zaddie became a millionaire many times over.

Although Zaddie had become quite wealthy, her need to work hard never abated. In spite of all her money and prestige, every morning when at home, she would sweep the walks in front of the Village Pharmacy and the two theatres. Those properties belonged to her, and she was determined that they would be clean and in good repair.

It must be obvious as to the reasons for my choice of Zaddie Bunker to be a part of "Before Their Time - Women Who Dared". She was born in 1887 and died one week shy of her 82nd birthday in February, 1969. During those 82 years, this colorful woman became an icon for girls and women throughout the country. Her daring-do exploits inspired other females to challenge the established culture and strictures of that time. Women over those years had been making slow progress, to be sure; yet the barriers were still difficult and daunting. Women could not vote when she was young; women were expected to stay at home and not work outside of a marriage; women were not supposed to be making decisions about investments and how to spend money; women were not expected to become millionaires on their own merit. Zaddie simply did not recognize that there was a barrier.

She was a visionary who recognized the potential in a remote desert area and helped to transform it into the world-famous Palm Springs. What she aspired to, she did. Whatever she attempted, she was successful. Zaddie was a daredevil.

She dared her own limitations, she dared the times she lived in, and she dared to take on the male establishment in the worlds of mechanics, chauffeuring, piloting, plus the business world. In all her endeavors she soared higher than her plane could ever take her.

Zaddie Bunker was a unique and amazing woman who tackled every challenge with skill and determination. She was always ahead of her time.

ZADDY BUNKER

KITTY O'NEIL

"As one goes through life, one learns that if you don't paddle
your own canoe, you don't move…"
—Katherine Hepburn

The final remarkable woman I write about is Kitty O'Neil, a truly incredible being who was a role model for women, for men and for the handicapped. I am reluctant to use the word "handicapped" because Kitty did not consider herself to be so labeled. She always felt that any barrier, whether of body, mind or spirit, was simply another challenge to overcome. She never felt held back by the fact that she was completely deaf and had been since infancy.

Ordinarily, a person who was female, petite, fought cancer twice, contacted spinal meningitis, had no father, was almost fatally injured in a crash, was born and raised on an Indian Reservation by her Cherokee mother and was deaf would have considered themselves handicapped by poverty, race, health and on-going struggles to communicate with others and would have buckled and been defeated from early childhood. Not Kitty O'Neil – not ever.

Before I begin her courageous story, I must give much credit to her mother, who was also way ahead of her time. Kitty's mother, Patsy Linn Compton O'Neil, also lived a courageous and unusual life. Patsy was born in 1917 and raised in the Muskogee Indian Territory. She was a member of the Cherokee people, thus making Kitty a Cherokee as well. The Cherokee Indian Tribe has a fascinating history. It was and is primarily a matriarchal tribe. The women of the tribe owned the land and the homes. They were considered to be the wise counsel on tribal matters and even fought in battles in early times. They were endowed with a sense of personal and tribal power. If a Cherokee woman married outside the tribe, the children were considered to be Cherokee with all the rights that the tribe practiced. If a Cherokee man married outside the tribe, his children would not be considered Cherokee and must live off the tribal lands and have no rights as a tribal member.

This is significant because Kitty's mother, Patsy Linn Compton, was the child of John O'Neil, an oil wildcatter who joined the U.S. Air Force during World War II. John was born in 1917 in Oklahoma. A white man, he somehow met her mother, Patsy, and they married. Because it was Patsy who had the power in her Cherokee nation, he was accepted by the tribe. The young couple had Kitty on March 24, 1946 in Corpus Christi, Texas while John was serving in the U.S. Air Force. Shortly after Kitty's birth, her father died in a plane crash, leaving her mother, Patsy, to raise two young children alone.

Native Americans, then and now, have been stereotyped, mistreated, robbed of their culture and their land, treated as inferior and subjected to racism. Much like Black slaves, they had no laws to protect them against the theft of their heritage, their culture and their land. Nevertheless, Kitty's mother was indomitable. She had been a college student when she met John O'Neil. This alone was unique because the Native American elementary and secondary schools were notoriously bad, and yet she made it into college. After her husband's death, Patsy worked, enrolled in college part time and graduated, eventually becoming a speech therapist. She also co-founded a school for students with hearing impairment in Wichita Falls, Texas.

Patsy was so passionate about helping those who were deaf because, when Kitty was five months old, she contracted measles and mumps simultaneously. This combination of childhood illnesses often causes deafness. Kitty at five months of age was profoundly deaf.

Patsy O'Neil was determined to help her child communicate. On her own and with no knowledge at that time of what to do for a deaf child, she taught Kitty lip-reading and speech. Patsy prepared for that task by taking education courses at The University of Texas. She graduated and with her knowledge, then taught many other deaf children. She home schooled Kitty until she was eight years old. Kitty was able to be enrolled in 3rd grade in a regular public school because she had become proficient at speech, thanks to her mother. Patsy Compton was, indeed, a powerhouse who mastered and overcame all her own challenges and triumphed as a mother, a scholar, a deaf advocate and a woman.

Kitty O'Neil seemingly inherited all the courage and power of her mother. She grew up, deaf, but was never defeated or fearful. Her life and accomplishments are the subject of this chapter.

As a deaf child, Kitty remarkably learned to play the cello and the piano. She did this by sensing subtle changes in the frequency of the vibrations. She learned voice modulation by feeling another person's vocal vibrations and then matching them using her own voice. The goal was to reduce the high pitch that typifies deaf speech.

At the age of twelve, Kitty joined a swim team which led to an interest in diving. As a substitute for a diver who failed to show up, Kitty, who had never previously dived, won the first-place medal. She then became a competitive 10-meter platform diver and 3-meter springboard diver. She won the Amateur Athletic Union Diving championship. Six months later, she had won the AAU Southwest District Junior meet.

These feats brought her to the attention of a famous diving coach, Sammy Lee, the first Asian American man to win an Olympic gold medal for the United States, who offered to train her. Patsy moved Kitty and her brother to Anaheim, California, so Kitty could train to be a competitor in the 1964 Olympics. She spent four hours a day in the water, and she was named Youth Athlete of the Month by the American Youth Magazine. She won the 10-meter diving event at the 1964 AAU Nationals. Sammy Lee once commented that she "snapped up trophies like a hungry fish."

Once again, fate dealt her a blow. Before the Olympic trials, she broke her wrist and then contracted spinal meningitis which threatened her ability to walk. In fact, it was illness, not injury, that often derailed her determination to be the best at any sport she competed in. At one point it looked as if she would never walk again, but her determination once again prevailed and she recovered.

Although her Olympic dreams were shattered, by the following year, 1965, she had pushed through the pain and relearned to walk well. She then competed in the 100m backstroke and 100m freestyle swimming at the 1965 Summer Deaflympics. She stated that diving "was not scary enough for me". She then started mastering new skills and began to compete in water skiing, scuba diving, skydiving and hang gliding. In all of these she excelled and won awards.

Five years later, in 1970, she took up racing on land and water. On water, she set the world records for speed in a jet-powered boat called Captain Crazy at 275 mph. She also set the world record on water skis at 105 mph. These speed records were, then and now, unparalleled. She was in her early 20's.

In her late 20's and early 30's, she was twice diagnosed with cancer. She fought back the disease both times and continued to live her life of absolute daring. It is impossible to guess why she was so strong, so determined and could survive and thrive after so many serious injuries and illnesses. She gave a partial answer herself in an interview with People magazine in 1977: My mother pushed me to read lips, but she didn't push me in sports. I did that myself. Because I was deaf, I had a very positive mental attitude. You have to show people you can do anything." She was always trying to prove her self-worth so as not to be judged by others.

For Kitty, being deaf gave her the spur to achieve more, not less. She always believed that her size helped. She was 5'2" tall and weighed just 97 lbs. Because she was light and quick, she stated that she was better able to withstand the hard-landing and frequent impacts which were a part of a life dedicated to high-risk sports. What is self-evident is the fact that she was fairly impervious to pain and just naturally fearless. In 2015 she told a reporter, "I'm not afraid of anything. Just do it. It feels good when you finish. You made it."

For Kitty, the next exciting challenge was cross country motorcycle racing and automobile racing. Racing became her greatest love – speed was what motivated her. Kitty gained the title of the fastest woman in the world on December 6, 1976 when she set a land-speed record in a 48,000-horsepower hydrogen peroxide-powered, three-wheeled rocked car called the Motivator. The Motivator, built by Bill Fredrick, was valued at $350,000 (equivalent to $1.7 million dollars in 2021).

She tore through the dry lake bed at Alford Desert in Oregon at an average speed of 512.71 mph with a peak speed of 621 mph. This record stood until 2019 when it was broken by Jessi Combs. He broke the record but died in the attempt. Kitty lived on to perform even more death-defying acts of bravery.

In one motorbike event, the off-road race, the Mint 400, she was in an accident. She got up, peeled off her gloves and found two severed fingers left inside. A fellow racer, Duffy Hambleton, came to her aid and insisted on taking her to a hospital to have them reattached. A four-hour surgery, followed by intense physical therapy allowed her to regain full use of that injured left hand. She was able once again to play the piano.

It was reported that Kitty later married Duffy Hambleton, but this was never substantiated. If so, it would have been a very short marriage, as he only showed up in her life for a short time. In 1988 she showed a reporter her scrapbooks and in one picture of her "husband" his face was scratched out. She had written "not true" next to a clipping about how he had influenced her work.

In the mid-1970's, when Kitty was in her late 20's and early 30's, she became a stunt woman for the movie industry. She trained with Hal Needham, Duffy Hambleton and Dar Robinson, three of the greatest stuntmen of the time. In 1976, she became the first woman admitted into the Hollywood Daredevil Team, Stunts Unlimited. As a stuntwoman, she appeared in the films The Bionic Woman, Airport '77, The Blues Brothers, Smokey and the Bandit II, plus many other television and film productions. She and Jeannie Epper were both stunt doubles for Lynda Carter in numerous episodes of Wonder Woman in 1976. Kitty was also a stunt double for Lindsay Wagner in many episodes of The Bionic Woman, also in 1976.

Women had performed as stand- ins for Hollywood films since the first movies were filmed, but were never allowed to do dangerous stunts. Men dominated the field and the men regularly doubled for female actresses to do the more dangerous stunts. There were no official training or safety requirements until 1961 when the Stuntmen's Association, after sustaining many injuries and some deaths, lobbied for safety standards.

In a 1979 episode of Wonder Woman, Kitty was hired to perform a stunt of extreme difficulty. She was asked to leap off of the 12-story Valley Hilton Hotel in Sherman Oaks, California into an inflatable air bag. In doing this dangerous stunt, she set a women's high-fall record of 127 feet.

Had she not landed in the precise center of that airbag, she would have died instantly. Once again, she defied the odds and did the stunt perfectly. She later broke her own high-fall record when she plunged out of a helicopter at 180 ft. At that height, she said the airbag looked like a postage stamp. Whatever Wonder Woman did on film, Kitty did for real. Withstanding fires, falls, crashes and explosions, she did every dangerous stunt asked of her. After Kitty's exploits, it was no longer possible to repeat the old bromide that women couldn't perform dangerous stunts.

In an NBC Special about the world's best stunt men and women, Kitty was featured tipping over a burning van, running with her clothes on fire and then falling over the edge of a seven-story parking garage. During filming, Kitty was required to remain in the van as firemen doused the walls of flames. The windshield had to be pulled off in order to extricate Kitty who was still strapped in the seat of the overturned van.

By now, Kitty was well known and acclaimed. However, everyone was not a fan. It was reported that a sponsor of a male stuntmen stated that it was "unbecoming and degrading for a woman to set a land speed record." He apparently was alone in his dismissal of her record-breaking, daredevil exploits and staggering achievements. In 1978, Mattel released a special edition Barbie doll action figure which was dressed in a yellow jumpsuit with a red scarf, like the ones Kitty wore on the race track.

Kitty became a star herself. In 1979 a biographical movie titled

"Silent Victory; the Kitty O'Neil Story" starring Stockard Channing was filmed. This was a made-for-TV biopic in which Kitty performed some of the stunts. She was also honored at the 91st Academy Awards in the Oscars' "In Memoriam" segment.

Kitty retired in 1986 because she felt burned out physically and mentally after seeing so many of her colleagues injured or killed in the line of work. She moved to Eureka, South Dakota where her peaceful home overlooked Lake Eureka. She lived there with her long-time companion, Raymond Wald. When asked why she retired, she said it was not because of fear, but because two of her friends had been killed while performing stunts. In Eureka, Kitty spent much of her time supporting the American Cancer Society's efforts against breast cancer. A quarter of the local museum in Eureka is devoted to housing artifacts from her remarkable career.

Kitty O'Neil died of pneumonia on November 2, 2018 at the age of 72.

In spite of all this publicity, I had not personally heard her amazing story until my son-in-law, Dave, read something of her world-renowned speed records and brought her to my attention. I was stunned to learn of this woman who had held 22 world records while overcoming deafness, near-fatal accidents, debilitating illnesses, racism and sexism. Kitty did unbelievable things in her lifetime. Hopefully, more people will be inspired from learning of Kitty O'Neal's unique life.

"If you obey all the rules you miss all the fun…"
—*Katherine Hepburn*

KITTY O'NEIL

THE WOMEN PIRATES

"Under a black flag we sail and the sea shall be our empire"
—Unknown

I cannot end this book without giving a nod to the most controversial of subjects – the women pirates. Yes, there were actually women pirates, and they were the fiercest of the women of any time period. I was intrigued when my daughter, Tracy Folks, told me that there were approximately ten women who had lived this dangerous and vicious life. The two most famous (or infamous) of these pirates was Anne Bonny born in 1697 in Old Head of Kinsale, Ireland, and Mary Read, alias Mark Reed, whose mother passed her daughter off as Mark in order to get a widow's pension.

The other five women written about in the previous pages of this book were each exceptional in their strength of character, their determination, their intelligence and their personal power. Each was successful in their life endeavors and became role models for the generations of women whose lives they touched. Nefertiti, Elizabeth Ann Fuller, Mary Ellen Pleasant, Zaddie Bunker and Kitty O'Neal were positive role models. Women pirates were not icons and certainly not role models.

I was very conflicted about even acknowledging women pirates. After all, they had taken on the worst of bad male behaviors. The two I am writing about killed many people – not just other pirates, but working sailors and passengers riding on the ships these women boarded in order to loot cargo and steal everything of value. And yet------there is a story behind these crimes; lives in which the only experiences were deprivation and violence. Those stories are not an excuse for their terrible actions, but provides the background to help open the door to understanding the "why" of their behavior, AND, a possible understanding of the world in which they were born and lived.

In that world, once again, women were generally powerless; and, if poor, had to scramble to survive. These women assumed the mantle of male pirates of the day who were angry, desperate and ruthless in their determination to seize whatever they could in order to create a sense of personal power.

PRIVATEERS vs. PIRATES: Furthermore, there is a paradox regarding the role of governments of the leading countries at that time. Although there are still pirates operating along the coasts of many countries today, privateers (a.k.a., buccaneers) and pirates infamously operated primarily during the 17th and 18th centuries.

Although privateers and pirates are terms used interchangeably, they are quite different. Their lives were blurred between those two very different terms. Most pirates of the 1600's and 1700's started their lives of crime as privateers who were actually pirates with legal papers. Private individuals who owned an armed ship could obtain a government commission which provided government authorization to use these ships during war. Thus, they were sanctioned to capture enemy merchant ships and carry out quasi-military activities. These privately-owned ships not only robbed merchant vessels, but they pillaged settlements of rival countries. The governments sponsoring this coastal raiding which included robbery, kidnapping and murder apparently had no qualms about the carnage as they considered it the cost of war.

Once peace was negotiated between the warring countries, privateers had no further role; and in order to continue their lucrative work, they became known as pirates and were now labeled criminals.

There were ten known women pirates, sometimes married to pirates, who were, like the men, opportunists. All of these pirates must have felt betrayed by their sponsoring governments. They continued the only lives they had known and were now labeled as criminals. The two women pirates I have selected to write about, Anne Bonny and Mary Read (alias Mark Reed) were part of this legal/illegal trade and paid the price for the governments' reversal of commitment to the privateers. This is what I have gleaned about their hard lives.

ANNE BONNY: There are different accounts of Anne Bonny's birth and life. One account stated that Anne was the illegitimate and headstrong daughter of an Irish lawyer from South Carolina. Another account stated that Anne was born in 1697 in Old Head of Kinsale, Count Cork, Ireland, an impoverished area. Some accounts appear to state that Anne's birth name was Bonny; other accounts do not show her birth name but state that she met and married a James Bonny, a common seaman. I could not ascertain whether her maiden name was Bonny, or if Bonny was a married name.

What seems to be accepted is that she married a seaman and ran off with him. When he decided that there was more money in piracy, he joined a pirate ship, Anne then disguised herself as a man and joined the crew with her husband. This marriage was short-lived because in May of 1719, their pirate ship landed in New Providence, Rhode Island where Anne met "Calico" Jack Rackham, a pirate captain. She abandoned her husband and boarded "Calico" Jack's stolen ship as his mistress. Anne joined his crew disguised as a man.

MARY READ: Mary joined Captain Calico Jack's crew in a different way. She was also illegitimately born in either England or Ireland. Her mother and been married and had a stillborn boy. Her mother had also had an affair and bore Mary later. She dressed Mary as a boy from infancy in order to pass her off as the son from her former marriage. A relative, believing that this child was related, gave a stipend to support the mother and child. They were still impoverished but able to survive.

Thus, Mary Read, known by all as Mark Reed, never knew life as a girl. She was always treated and acknowledged as a male. When she was a teenager, Mary first worked in domestic service, once again as a male. Wanting a better life, she/he signed up to join the navy but ran away to join the army. She was in the infantry and sent to the Netherlands where she met a messmate to whom she revealed her secret. They quietly married, but she still lived in disguise

Mary Read/Mark Reed's bad-luck life did not alter; her secret husband died shortly after the marriage. Still living in male clothing, she joined a Dutch ship as a seaman and sailed for the West Indies. When the ship approached the Americas, English pirates attacked and boarded the Dutch ship.

Apparently, because Mary was the only crew member to speak English, the British pirates thought she was a boy who was from their country. Believing she was a young boy and might have been commandeered, they allowed her/him to join their crew. When the English pirate ship arrived in New Providence, Mary jumped ship to also join "Calico" Jack Rackham's ship which was leaving for Cuba. Sometime during this voyage, the two women recognized each other's disguises and started collaborating.

Formerly, a pirate crewman, "Calico" Jack Rackham became a pirate captain when he stole a sloop named "William" after his former captain, Charles Vane, was captured and executed. There were only nine crew members on the stolen sloop, "William". They were a rowdy and drunken crew. "Calico" only lasted about eight months as a pirate captain.

One night in late 1720, the crew were sleeping off a drunken night when a Royal Navy ship dropped anchor close by and boarded the "William". According to later testimony at their trial, the two women tried to rouse the drunken crew from their stupor, but it was reported that only Anne Bonny and Mary Read fought back and offered resistance.

"Calico" Jack Rackham was never well known as a pirate captain until he and his crew were captured. He became famous only because it was discovered that two of his crew were women. This caused a sensation at the time because most seaman believed that a woman on board was bad luck. Women captives were thrown overboard because of this superstition. The fact that Anne Bonny and Mary Read had been living on board disguised as men caused much publicity and scrutiny about the world of the pirates. The two women became famous.

After their capture, "Calico" Jack and the crew were taken to Port Royal to stand trial. At the trial, different crewmen gave different testimony. Some accounts stated that the two women only dressed as men when they were acting as pirates, while dressing and behaving as women when they were not raiding, boarding ships or fighting. Other crew reported that they always pretended to be men and never revealed themselves as women. It was also reported that both women had crewmen as lovers. What was fantasy, wishful thinking or truth will never be known. "Calico" Jack Rackham and his male crew were all hanged on November 27, 1720.

Anne Bonny and Mary Read were condemned but spared because they both pleaded that they were pregnant. Mary was taken to a Jamaican prison in 1721. Still supposedly pregnant, she died in prison of a fever. Anne apparently was either let out of prison or escaped because records show that she died on April 22, 1782 in South Carolina. If so, she would have been 85 years old. Apparently, she left the world of piracy for a quieter life in South Carolina.

Whatever dire circumstances led these two women to a life of piracy, we may never know or understand. They were willing criminals; however, most criminals resort to crime because their lives are so damaged and their future so dismal, that they see no possibility of survival in their poverty-stricken world. Both the life of a government-sanctioned buccaneer, and the life of a hunted criminal were fraught with hardship and with danger. Both Anne Bonny and Mary Read were not forced into these lives; they willingly entered them. Why? To gain power? To become independent? To escape the existence demanded of women?

The lives of women in the 1600's and 1700's was one of submission; and, if poor and illegitimate, degradation. Females were literally the property of the men in their lives. The laws and standards of the time demanded that women play their proscribed roles as helpmates only. No physical or intellectual freedom was open to them. So, perhaps, these pirate women made the decision to grab whatever limited freedom was allowed to men. They dressed as men; they fought as men; they lived as men.

Life was harsh; and if captured, death was certain. However, they had excitement, adventure, money and a sense of power. Their criminal actions were abhorrent, but they were <u>way</u> ahead of their time in demanding that they had the right to seek what they wanted and needed. Their courage was evident in the dangerous lives they lived. Their daring deeds still amaze. These women pirates were ahead of their time, and they dared to refuse the roles demanded of women of the time.

"If you ship doesn't come in, swim out to it."
—*Jonathan Winters*

PIRATE GIRL

CONCLUSION

─────────

"Never believe that a few caring people can't change the world.
"For, indeed, that's all who ever have."

—*Margaret Mead*

─────────

The women highlighted in this book epitomized determination, courage and daring. Their actions and exploits became a heritage for all of us who followed.

So, what have women achieved since these women dared to be daring? Women have demanded and won the vote, risen to the top in the corporate world, been elected to local, state and national offices, become writers, artists and small business owners. They have also raised sons who understand that marriage is a partnership, not a dictatorship. Those women excelled at leadership and motherhood. How does one encapsulate such free spirits in limited words?

There is a very long and arduous journey from Nefertiti's life 3,700 years ago to the life of Kitty O'Neil who died in 2018. There were and are many who met the criteria of "ahead of their time" and "daring". The women in this book magically came to my attention through others who admired these unique individuals. The women in these pages ventured far ahead of the expectations of those, mostly men, who were in charge during their lifetimes. These women had to be aware of their vulnerability and the danger of defying the power structure of their time.

In their lifetimes, each ventured far ahead of the expectations of those, mostly men, who were in charge. Were the women aware of their vulnerability and the danger of defying the power structure of their time? Of course, they were, and yet they defied the law and rule makers. As challenging as this may have been, these women never retreated in fear. Whatever barriers they had to overcome, their innate abilities and intelligence drove them to achieve what others could not. They were never the "lesser" sex!

I was first inspired by Elizabeth Ann Fuller. I am an amateur, but prolific genealogist who has been working on my family tree for over thirty years. I discovered Elizabeth Ann, who was my 11th great grandmother and was intrigued by her actions as described in her mini-bio in Chapter two.

For years, I talked with family members about this unusual woman. Over time, thoughts of her daring kept recurring to me. I knew I needed to honor this unique ancestress, but I also knew I did not know enough of her life to fill a book. A friend suggested writing about other women lost in history who also needed their stories told. How was I to discover these other amazing women? I need not have been concerned. They found me.

Here I must digress and acknowledge and praise the millions and millions of women who did not lead lives of "daring". Their quiet lives and quiet deaths also shaped the future of both men and women. Un-lauded and under-appreciated, most women throughout history have performed their assigned tasks while also influencing and inspiring their children and grandchildren to lead good and honorable lives. It is rare when a successful person does not acknowledge some woman who was there to encourage, guide and smooth their path toward success. Indeed, these "influencers" exist in most lives; mothers, grandmothers, daughters, sisters, aunts, teachers who have influenced, shaped and molded those fortunate enough to be in their orbit. These women are "believers". They believe in themselves, and they believe in those they guide. They not only encourage talents and abilities, they encourage those they love to seek untrodden paths, to dream, to plan, to fail and learn from that failure. They urge others to DO. We thrive under their loving guidance. With them, we KNOW we are smart, talented and creative.

"Not all of us can do great things, but we can do small things with great love."

—*MOTHER TERESA*

Many years ago, my two sons, Scott and Brent, gave me a much-treasured plaque with this poem written by a very wise woman, Barbara Burrow. Her words still resonated as I wrote this book because it is so true of those who lived the daring life and those who lived the quiet life.

That Woman is a Success...
who loves life
and lives it to the fullest
who has discovered and shared
the strengths and talents
that are uniquely her own;
who puts her best into each task
and leaves each situation
better than she found it;
who seeks and finds
that which is beautiful
in all people...and all things;
whose heart is full of love
and warm with compassion;
who has found joy in living
and peace within herself.

I also want to pay tribute to the enlightened men throughout the world who value and support the women in their lives who are emancipated. Although I have written primarily about the repressive men, I am encouraged by the vast numbers of evolved men who stand up in every way for women's equality. It must be difficult for these determined men to resist the old male culture of suppression of women. They not only support women's struggles for equality, but, they march, they speak up, they rally support. I applaud them for their actions and their courage.

I, myself, was married to two wonderful men who supported and encouraged my beliefs and passion for equality. My two sons, my son-in-law and my two grandsons are equally free from the fear of strong women. Indeed, they choose them. In addition, I am fortunate to have found male friends who prefer the company of women who demand respect.

Having acknowledged that many men have evolved as much as women, I must share one of my favorite Christmas gifts which I found hilarious and fundamentally true. This was written by some brilliant woman and quoted on a tea towel given to me as a gift. The three Wise Men of the Christmas story are satirized thus;

> *Three Wise Women*
> *would have*
> *asked directions,*
> *arrived on time,*
> *helped deliver the baby,*
> *cleaned the stables,*
> *made a casserole,*
> *brought practical gifts…*
> *and there would be*
> *Peace on Earth!*

As for myself, my journey to full participation in the world of work, political activism, relationships and mode of living has been a winding path. Born and raised in the Midwest, the Bible Belt, I was inculcated with the belief that I must follow the dictates of my father and emulate my mother who was raised by parents from the Victorian era. My mother was a believer in the idea that women needed to play the housewife/helpmate role. In addition to my parents as role models, there was my church, my schools and my friends and their families who all subscribed to the same beliefs in women's roles. I never once heard an argument against these prescribed, subservient rules for women as dictated by society.

I was, however, a reader; and by my teen years I was hesitant, but determined to ask the hard question: Why? Although my family was poor, with scholarships and part-time jobs, I was able to attend and graduate from Indiana University where some of those questions were answered. After graduation, my fiancé and I married in the small college chapel and left immediately for California. I have only visited my old home area since. We never returned permanently.

In California, I discovered a different culture, a different mindset. I was able to explore my curiosity and began the journey toward understanding. I began my evolution toward the hated word, "feminism". By the early 1970's, I had joined the National Organization for Women (N.O.W.) which is regarded as one of the main liberal feminist organizations in the United States.

NOW lobbies for economic and constitutional equality. It also campaigns for reproductive rights, racial rights and LGBTQIA rights. It was the second wave of feminist demands for justice and was founded by Betty Friedan, a feminist author and activist. Along with Shirley Chisholm and other brilliant activists, these feminists laid the groundwork for much of the progress of women's rights. Much has already been written about them.

As a NOW member, I entered a circle of women who also chafed at the restrictiveness inherent in the society of the 1960's and 1970's. It was a liberating and exciting time. Eventually, it led to this book. So, my gratitude toward all women -- those who led the quiet lives and those who dared. I am proud to be a part of the female half of the human race.

The question still arises: Has female equality been achieved? No! Throughout the world, there are still societies which demand that women act and live in the same way as women did over many thousands of years. In other words, they are refused educations, they are the property of the men in their lives. Women in those countries have no legal rights, and they live in fear of reprisal if they dare object.

China, in the 1970's was extremely concerned about over-population; so, in 1979, they passed a law to curb population growth. It was called the one-child initiative, and it led to disastrous results. Chinese culture throughout history had patriarchal expectations and preference for sons.

By Confucian tradition, Chinese sons are obligated to care for their elderly parents. Daughters had their husbands chosen by their parents, and those daughters were then to switch their allegiance to the husband's parents and family. They were then to care for their spouse's parents, not their own.

Enforcement of the one-child law varied due to region and social status, but there were large fines and other penalties for women who became pregnant a second time. Careful records were kept on every woman, and those documents were very invasive as were the procedures. Menstrual cycles, contraceptive usage and past births were kept on record by local officials.

With one child, healthcare subsidies, retirement funds and larger grain allowances were provided. If a mother became pregnant with a second child, they lost all these benefits. For the poor, this would have been disastrous. Local officials could make the woman abort the baby, or she could be sterilized. In some cases, I.U.D.'s were involuntarily inserted into child-bearing women. There was a huge campaign to urge females to marry later in life. They were also given mandatory blood tests to determine pregnancy. Ultrasounds became very popular because the sex of the infant could be determined, which led to abortions of baby girls. If born, females were often abandoned, sent to orphanages or adopted abroad. When the government closed the adoption loophole, two million Chinese baby girls were abandoned. The greatest tragedy was the huge number of girls killed at birth. Their tiny bodies were found abandoned throughout the nation.

China claims it prevented 400 million births which is disputed by some. By the late 1990's and early 2000's, it became the generation of the "missing women". There was a deficit of 40 million female babies, and there were 30 million more men than women by 2020. By 2015, the Chinese government realized that there were not enough young girls for the all the boys who escaped the fate of their sisters. The law was then altered to allow each family two children. By 2021, three children were allowed; and later in 2021 there were no restrictions on family size. Nevertheless, small families are now the preference and boys are still favored. Infanticide still exists in China, and it is still little girls who are sacrificed.

Was the Western world more compassionate toward women? Read any newspaper or listen to any news broadcast, and you will still hear of the horrors visited on the women in their society.

America has its own dark past. The Salem Witch Trials which have been described as a kind of mass hysteria were one of the dark chapters in our history. Salem, Massachusetts in the late 16th and 17th centuries was largely settled and governed by Puritans. Although this conservative religion dominated the lives of the Puritans, the general population was widely known to have family feuds, quarrels with neighbors and even fellow church attendees and church leaders.

Salem's inhabitants were a quarrelsome lot arguing over church beliefs, property lines and grazing rights. Puritan women were considered to be inherently sinful, weak and susceptible to the appeal of the Devil. They were deemed more accepting than men to the temptations offered by a secular world run by the Devil.

Although some men were accused and tried for witchcraft, 78% of the accused were women. Many of the men accused were husbands or relatives of the accused women. The men were guilty because they claimed that their women were innocent. The accusers of the women often had previously quarreled with those they claimed to be witches. If the woman was unmarried or childless, it was quite common to accuse her of witchcraft. The so-called witch trials were shams. Guilt could be established if the "witch" had moles or birth marks which the accusers said was an indication that the devil drank their blood. One woman was on trial because her clothes were often black and were deemed "awkward" and against Puritan styles. She was found guilty and hanged. One small girl, 4 years old, was accused of witchcraft. Her mother was found guilty of guiding her child toward witchcraft.

From February, 1692 to May, 1693, 200 people were accused, 30 found guilty, 19 hanged on Gallows Hill (14 women, 5 men). Fourteen other women and two men had been executed in other parts of Massachusetts and Connecticut during the 17th Century. Some women confessed to the crime in order to live. Five others died in jail, and one man who refused to plead at all was pressed to death by adding ever heavier stones to his chest until it crushed his lungs. Even those who were freed had their lives ruined, property confiscated and families shamed and expelled from their churches. Tens of thousands of lives were impacted and ruined by these church-going believers in witchcraft.

Present-day Americans feel relieved that we do not live under such repressive laws. Yet, today, conservative male legislators still block the Equal Rights Amendment and its push to pay women the same amount as men doing the very same work. More and more state legislators are still attempting to encroach on the hard-fought gains that women have made over hundreds of years.

Are we defeated? Never! Women of strength, determination and power will continue to resist being boxed in by old-world expectations. Those still entrenched in the fear of women's intelligence and power will always attempt to "keep us in our place". Our place, in their minds, will always be in subservient roles to themselves. Will women of today submit to this fear and pressure? Absolutely not!

Women have come too far, know too much AND have gained the knowledge of how to win. The difference between 3,700 years ago and the present is NUMBERS. There were few women who dared defy the laws, rules and societal pressure of the past. Today, there are too many young women of education and determination who have economic and political power. They will not submit to unfair and unrealistic goals from an old-world order. Numbers equal power, and the numbers are ever-growing.

As for those men (and some women) who still fear women's progress toward true equality, tell them to rest easy. Eroding the old ways of thinking and behaving will improve all ways of life. An equal partner, instead of a live-in worker, will provide more freedom for both partners. Women of today yearn only for the autonomy, dignity, freedom and equality that men demand for themselves.

As repeatedly emphasized, the oppression of women and girls is still a world-wide problem demanding perseverance, determination and self-sacrifice by all the women's rights movements. Women are still commonly devalued, and the on-going battle for gender equality slogs on. Female leaders are well aware of the need for laws to enforce their rights, but too many men cling to their belief in the stereotypical "weaker" sex, and fear the economic fallout if women become their true equals.

The powerful women of the past and of today have always been aware of their vulnerability, and the danger of defying the power structure they struggle against. Do we still experience fear and doubt? Of course, we all worry and fear retribution and judgment. Yet, our knowledge of our innate abilities and intelligence will drive us to find what those in the past could rarely achieve – true equality.

The women highlighted in this small volume do not stand alone in history's changing treatment of women. Every culture, every ethnicity, every historical time and every country has had its share of self-liberated women who lived lives outside the norms of their time. Each succeeding generation stands on the shoulders of those who dared. We seek their courage to continue to break the bonds of our individual society's cultural expectations and demands. Both women and men will benefit when full equality is achieved.

> *"When we are no longer able to change a situation – we are challenged to change ourselves"*
> —*Viktor. E. Frankl*

Dare to change yourself and let the world discover the unique and special talents and abilities you have brought to our troubled world. It is your gift to future generations.

Shirley Wells

ACKNOWLEDGEMENTS

In my long lifetime, I have been supported and cherished by many loved ones, especially my wonderful sisters, Carol Sweeney and Marilyn Breedlove.

However, I shall now acknowledge only those who have directly impacted the writing of this small book.

First and foremost: TRACY RUGE-FOLKS, my daughter, who proof-read, edited, inspired the Pirate chapter, and created the art work and design for this book.

Also, these others provided valuable material and inspiration. Thank you to:

Brad Geagley for the introduction to and research on Mary Ellen Pleasant.

Dave Folks for leading me to Kitty O'Neil and providing the photography magic.

Edie Bymel Ruge for her advice on Neanderthals and her on-going support.

Yvette Altman for her corrections and general critique.

AND, for my loved ones who encouraged and believed in my interest and ability:

Sons: Scott and Brent Ruge

Grandchildren: Ryan, Jacqueline, Taylor and Casey Ruge

Special ones: Bryan Mootz, Bryan Overmeyer, Melissa Ruge and Ian Raveschot

ABOUT THE AUTHOR

Shirley H. Wells has a. Bachelor of Science (B.S.) degree and a Master of. Arts (M.A.) degree. She has been an English teacher, Dean of Girls. Assistant Principal, Principal, District Coordinator, Director of Alternative Education and Director of Court School Programs. She has also been a lecturer in several colleges. She was a field representative for the U.S. Department of Justice with the National School Safety Center. She was a consultant and trainer for the California State Department of Education, probation and police departments, school districts and county offices of education. She has made numerous presentations on juvenile delinquency, discipline, prevention, intervention and business-education partnerships. Ms. Wells received commendations from the California Governor's Office, the California Legislature, boards of supervisors, school boards and the California Department of Education. She is author of a previous book ("Who Do You Think You Are?"), plus two articles on drug education in professional publications. She is retired, widowed and the mother of three children, four grandchildren and two great grandchildren.

Printed in the United States
by Baker & Taylor Publisher Services